AKHBAR MECCA

Muḥammad ibn ʿAbd Allah al-Azraqi

Akhbar Mecca
An English Translation, 1 to 156

Muḥammad ibn ʿAbd Allah al-Azraqi

Presented by Dan Gibson

2026

Independent Scholar's Press

Akhbar Mecca
An English Translation, 1 to 156
by Muḥammad ibn ʿAbd Allah al-Azraqi

Copyright © 2026 Dan Gibson

ISP (Independent Scholar's Press is an imprint of CanBooks, Saskatoon, Canada). All rights reserved.

No part of this publication may be reproduced, stored in a retrieval system or transmitted in any form, by any means, electronic, mechanical, photocopying, recording or otherwise without the prior permission of the publishers, except in the case of brief quotations in critical articles or reviews.

Library of Congress Cataloging-in-Publication Data

Gibson, Daniel, 1956 –

ISBN: 978-1-927581-31-5

Table of Contents

Foreword	i
Introduction	iii
About the Translation	v
Acknowledgements	vi

Chapter One

The Creation of the Holy Ka'ba	1
The Origin of Tawaf	2
The Angels Visit the House	4
Adam's Ka'ba	5
The Supplication of Adam's Offspring and Tawaf Recitations	10
Allah Proclaims His Greatness to Adam	13
Seventy Thousand Angels Visit al-Bayt al-Ma'mour which is Ad-Dhuraah	15
Al-Bayt al-Ma'mour's Removal at the Time of the Flood	16
The Forbidden House Built by the Sons of Adam	17
Noah's Ark Circumambulates the House	17
Allah Shows Ibrahim the Position of the Ka'ba	17
Ibrahim Chooses the Location of the Ka'ba on Earth	18

Chapter Two

Jibril Reveals Zamzam and the Forbidden House to Hajar	19
The Arrival of the Jurhum and the Selection of Ismail's Wife	21
Ibrahim Builds the Ka'ba and Sets the Black Stone	23
Ibrahim Calls the World to Hajj and the Prophets Respond	31
The Ka'ba as the First House Established for Mankind	38
Ibrahim Makes Supplications; Allah Relocates Ta'if	39
The Descendants of Ismail	42
The Khuza'i Destroy the Jurhum and Change the Hanifiyyah	50

Chapter Three
The Responsibilities of Al-Siqayah, Al-Rifadah, and Al-Qiyadah . . . 59

Ismail's Progeny Turn to Idol Worship 67

Chapter Four
The Idol Hubal and Casting Lots by Arrows 69

Isaf and Nai'la Turned to Stone; The Destruction of the Quraysh's Idols . 70

Chapter Five
Amr ibn Luhi's Idols 75

The Idol Munat 75

Chapter Six
The Idols al-Lat and al-Uzzah 77

The Idol of Dhat-Anwat 79

Muḥammad Sends Troops to Demolish the Idols. 80

Tubba's Journey to the Ka'ba 81

The Habasha Attack al-Yaman 82

Abraha and the Elephant 83

Foreword

The work of al-Azraqi should have been translated into English a long time ago. Muḥammad ibn ʿAbd Allah al-Azraqi (محمـد بـن عبـد الله الأزرقـي) was an Islamic historian born in the second century AH, or ninth century CE. Azraqi published this work, *Akhbar Mecca* (which means "Information about Mecca"), in 251 AH (865 CE), making this text the third earliest extant history of Islam. While early when compared to other Muslim histories, *Akhbar Mecca* was still published 240 years after the death of Muḥammad—no history written during the first two centuries of Islamic history survives.

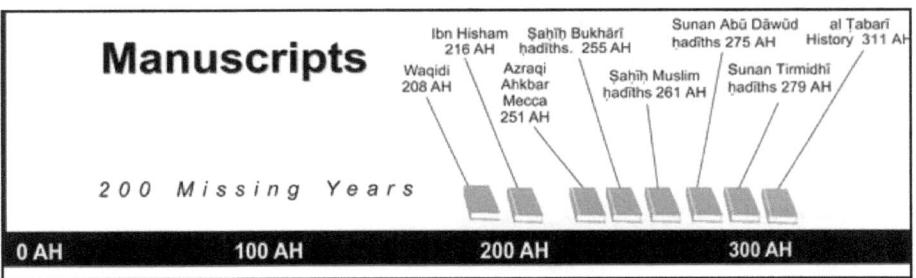

Azraqi's family had a long history in Mecca. As such, he was able to collect various accounts about Mecca and the Kaʿba from his family and acquaintances. Azraqi organized these accounts into a collection of various sayings, mostly attributed to Ibn Abbas, but sometimes attributed directly to Muḥammad. These accounts include *isnad*, or records of the transmission of the oral tradition, which help Muslim scholars to test the accounts' reliability.

The relative earliness of *Akhbar Mecca* already positions it as a crucial historical document. That it is so detailed and is a clear representation of how early Muslims understood their history and the holy Kaʿba only cements its importance.

I am the copyeditor and proofreader of this volume. I also copyedited and proofread Dan Gibson's 2023 book *Let the Stones Speak;* as such, I was introduced to the work of a variety of Islamic historians through Dan's research. I verified all of Dan's references to al-Tabari, al-Bukhari, and others, so I often spent considerable time paging through histories and hadith, reading passages to ensure the accuracy of our work.

I distinctly recall the importance of al-Azraqi to our argument. Since he is an early historian particularly focused on Mecca, *Akhbar Mecca* includes crucial information and provides a historical context to Dan's archaeological findings. For example, al-Azraqi's inclusion of the dimensions of the Kaʿba allowed Dan to identify the structure in Petra which suits the record remarkably.

I also distinctly remember asking Dan which English edition of al-Azraqi he used. It seemed obvious: surely the work of an Islamic historian this early, with this important a focus, would have been translated into English several times. It has not.

What follows is a text of necessity. Dan never intended for this project to be what it has become, so it has shortcomings. However, it is a worthy start. For the first time, a reasonable representation of the seminal work of al-Azraqi may be read by an English audience.

I recently spoke to a friend who is a PhD in history and Islamic studies. His exuberance when I explained this project was a tremendous encouragement to me. Some scholars will see the value of this work. Ordinary readers will gain a glimpse into Islamic history they would otherwise never see. The discourse is advanced.

Both Dan and I hope that this partial translation of *Akhbar Mecca* will encourage scholars to produce more precise and complete translations of the whole text. Perhaps there is an Arabic scholar out there who will abhor what we have done enough to do it right.

The beauty of this text, its insight, and its glimpse into a world shrouded by time is worth the trouble.

Chad Doell

Introduction

As I researched early Islamic history, I discovered that Muslims used a variety of qibla directions during the first three centuries of Islam. Scholarship has been slow to examine these findings, and even slower to accept them. This hesitancy is completely understandable as these discoveries question much of what we have learned about Islam from the ancient documents.

As I continued my research, I was surprised to realize that there was no modern English translation of the four volumes written by al-Azraqi. Their absence is a detriment to scholars who do not read Arabic because there are very few references to early Mecca outside of Azraqi. But, much like my own research and writings, modern scholarship has been reluctant to accept al-Azraqi. This reluctance, too, is understandable. Azraqi did not write for modern audiences who have come to expect certain modern standards. Rather, Azraqi tends to uncritically record the perspectives of his contemporaries without commentary.

He often writes "the people say..." to clarify that he is only recording what was said in his day or earlier, but he is careful not to personally identify with much of what he writes. Azraqi comments on his collection with a light hand and also seems to avoid certain controversies. These controversies may include the location of the original Mecca. Despite no direct commentary from the author on this issue, Azraqi's record is useful for finding indicators that something had happened with the location of Mecca. See, for example, several passages which describe how the settlement of Ta'if was miraculously relocated from the north to the south of Arabia (104-106 below).

The date of Azraqi's writing is also interesting. Having died in 837 CE, he was a contemporary of Ibn Hisham, who died in 833. This places him among the earlier Islamic writers, but strangely, he has been ignored by many.

What makes Azraqi different is that he does not write a general history of Islam or even of the prophet. Azraqi records what was known in his day of the city of Mecca and the Ka'ba structure. Azraqi's method of collecting all the information available to him, combined with the narrow scope of his record, means there are many details in his work which do not appear elsewhere.

Much of Azraqi's work in volume one focuses on the events before 70 AH (689 CE). When I produced a comprehensive database of early mosque qiblas, it became evident to me that all the mosques built during the time Azraqi writes about, faced the ancient city of Petra. I have argued elsewhere that the names used for Petra included the name Mecca[1] resulting in two locations bearing the same name. I believe

---

1. Dan Gibson, *Let the Stones Speak: Archaeology Challenges Islam* (Saskatoon: CanBooks, 2023), 98ff.

Azraqi must have written about the original city of Islam, known to us as Petra—but in his time bearing the name of Mecca.

This realization makes his book all the more interesting and may reveal why other Islamic scholars down through the ages never seemed too excited about Azraqi.

I trust that, in time, scholars who are better equipped to take on this task will produce a high-quality scholarly translation of all four volumes for the benefit of English language Islamic studies.

Dan Gibson

About the Translation

I never set out to put together an English version of Azraqi. If this was indeed my goal, I would have produced something that included all four volumes, with many in-depth notes. This text only includes the first 156 passages. I never had the time or finances to work on this project in detail, and so what follows is only a partial, practical, and rough translation of the first of four volumes of Azraqi.

The translation itself is not detailed or literal. Because Azraqi's work is so early, some of the word meanings are quite difficult to understand. More rigorous translation work needs to be done.

Text from the Qur'an and traditional Islamic liturgy appears in italics. References to the Qur'anic passages are provided. All Qur'anic quotations are from *The Study Quran: A New Translation and Commentary*, ed. Seyyed Hossein Nasr et al. (New York: Harper Collins, 2017).

The section headings which appear in some editions of Azraqi have been changed to better reflect the content of each section. Since these headings do not appear in early manuscripts of *Akhbar Mecca*, it seemed appropriate to adjust them. The section breaks, as well as passage numbers and chapter breaks, are retained.

Where it seems Azraqi was commenting on the text in his own voice, his comments are marked by (round brackets). Most of his comments add context or clarify pronouns. Words added by the translators and copyeditor appear in [square brackets]. Again, these additions usually provide clarity with pronouns, and sometimes include the Arabic word for particularly difficult words to translate.

An effort has been made to normalize the spelling of names across the *isnad* and in the body of the text. Since several assistant translators worked on the document, there may be inconsistences with the spelling of proper nouns. We apologize for this complication.

Finally, the reader will encounter interruptions to Azraqi's text, which appear in boxes throughout this book. These excursions provide context and notes of interest, particularly highlighting instances when Azraqi supports the archaeological evidence that demonstrates that Petra was the original Holy City of Islam.

Acknowledgements

As always, I must acknowledge those who have helped with this translation. Foremost is Iman Elmankush who labored a great deal on the initial manuscript. Second, I must acknowledge my wife who, as always, was helpful for understanding Arabic grammatical constructions and word meanings. Her experience with many dialects of Arabic across the Arabian Peninsula always proves valuable beyond measure. Mohammed H and Sohaib D must also be thanked for their work on the isnad. And as always, Chad Doell was there to find and catch all sorts of errors and omissions. This translation would not have been possible without everyone's efforts.

Dan Gibson

THE ENGLISH TRANSLATION OF AL-AZRAQI'S AKHBAR MECCA

VOLUME ONE

*In the name of Allah, The All-Merciful, The Ever-Merciful:
All Prayers and Blessings of Allah be upon the master of the nation, Muḥammad the prophet of mercy, and upon his family and companions.*

Chapter One

The Creation of the Holy Ka'ba

1 - My father, the jurist, Imam, and Hadith scholar, Sadr al-Din, the last of the sheikhs, Abu Hafs Umar ibn Abdul Majeed ibn Umar al-Qurashi al-Miyanshi, may Allah have mercy on him, informed me. He said, the judge, Imam Abu al-Muzaffar Muḥammad ibn Ali ibn al-Husayn al-Shaybani al-Tabari narrated to us on the authority of his grandfather, Sheikh Imam al-Husayn, on the authority of Sheikh Abu al-Hassan Ali ibn Khalaf al-Shami, on the authority of Abu al-Qasim Khalaf ibn Hibat Allah al-Shami, on the authority of Abu Muḥammad al-Hasan ibn Ahmad ibn Ibrahim ibn Firas, on the authority of Abu al-Hasan Muḥammad ibn Nafi' al-Khuza'i, on the authority of Abu Muḥammad Ishaq ibn Ahmad ibn Ishaq ibn Nafi' al-Khuza'i, on the authority of Abu al-Walid Muḥammad ibn Abdullah ibn Ahmad ibn Muḥammad ibn al-Walid ibn Uqba ibn al-Azraq ibn Amr ibn al-Harith ibn Abi Shamir al-Ghassani al-Azraqi, who said, my grandfather, Ahmad ibn Muḥammad ibn al-Walid al-Azraqi, narrated to us, saying, Sufyan ibn Uyayna narrated to us on the authority of Bishr ibn Asim, on the authority of Sa'id ibn al-Musayyib, who said that Ka'b al-Akhbar said:

"The Ka'ba was on a layer of froth above water, 40 years before Allah had created the skies and the earth, and from that froth the earth was created."

2 - He said, Abu al-Walid narrated to us, saying, Mahdi ibn Abi al-Mahdi narrated to me, saying, Abu Ayyub al-Basri narrated to us on the authority of Hisham, On the authority of Humayd, who said:

"I heard Mujahid say, 'Allah the Almighty created this house before he created the earth.'"

3 - He said, Abu al-Walid narrated to us, saying, my grandfather narrated to us on the authority of Sa'id ibn Salam, on the authority of Talhah ibn Amr, on the authority of Atta', on the authority of Ibn Abbas, that he said:

"When the Throne was above water, before the creation of the heavens and earth, Allah sent a quick wind which exposed a hard lump at the place of this house; it looked like a dome. Then Allah spread the earth underneath that position, and from there the earth stretched and stretched until Allah pegged it with mountains, and the first mountain that was created was Abu-Qubays. For that reason Mecca was called The Mother of Cities [Um al-Qura]."

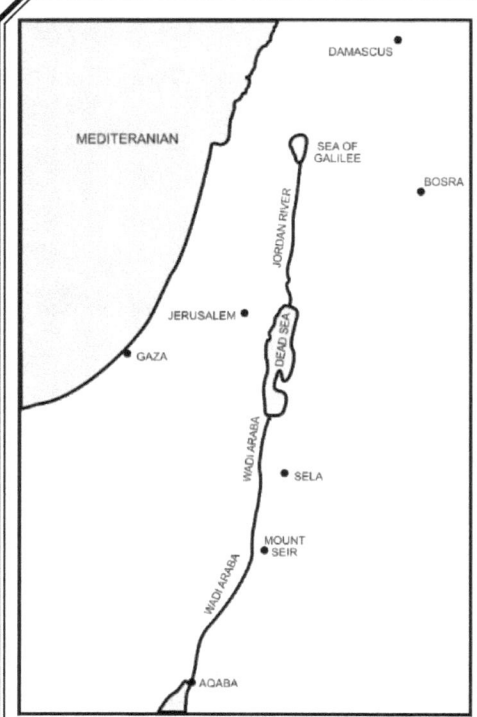

Sebeos, the Armenian Bishop and historian, lived during the Arab conquest and wrote that the Arabs "set out from the P'arhan desert" (Sebeos, Sebeos' History, trans. Robert Bedrosian, (New York: Public Domain, 1985), 40). Today many Muslims cite Sebeos as evidence that the prophet Muḥammad is mentioned in non-Islamic history, but they usually fail to note that Sebeos located the prophet Muḥammad and the founding of Islam in Paran, not in the Hijaz. The only major city near Paran was Mount Seir, known to the Roman west as Petra. Mount Seir is located 30.329858° 35.440244°.

Muslim scholars believe that the "Mother of Villages" (Um al-Qura) in Qur'an 6:92 refers to Mecca in the Hijaz. Gibson & Harremoës observed the Greek Byzantine Roman title for Petra translates as "Imperial Colony Antoniana Distinguished Holy *Mother of the Colonies* Hadriana Petra Metropolis of Tertia Palaestina Salutaris."[2]

4 - He said, Yahya ibn Sa'id narrated to me, on the authority of Muḥammad ibn Umar ibn Ibrahim al-Jubayri, on the authority of Uthman ibn Abdul Rahman, on the authority of Hisham, on the authority of Mujahid, who said:
"Allah the Almighty had created the position of this house two thousand years before the creation of earth, and its foundations are down in the seventh earth."

The Origin of Tawaf

5 - Abu al-Walid narrated to us, saying, Ali ibn Harun ibn Muslim al-Ajli narrated to me, on the authority of his father, who said, al-Qasim ibn Abdul Rahman al-Ansari narrated to us, saying, Muḥammad ibn Ali ibn al-Husayn narrated to me, saying:
"I was with my father Ali ibn al-Husayn in Mecca, and while he was doing tawaf [or circumambulation] and I was behind him, a tall man approached and put his hand

---

2. Traianos Gagos and Jaakko Frösén, "Petra Papyri," *Annual of the Department of Antiquities of Jordan* 42 (1998): 476.

on my father's back. My father turned around to see him, and the man said, 'peace be to you, son of the prophet's daughter; I want to ask you [a question].'

"My father did not reply to him and continued to finish the seven circles of tawaf while the man and I were behind him. When he finished his tawaf he entered al-Hijr [the enclosure of Ismail], and went under the Ka'ba's gutter, and prayed two Raka'at [liturgical prayers] after completing his tawaf. We prayed behind him, and then he settled in a seated position and I sat next to him. He said, 'Muḥammad, where is that questioner?' And I pointed to the man.

"He came and sat in front of my father. My father asked, 'what is your question?' He said, 'I am asking about the beginning of this tawaf at this house: why was it? And where was it? And when was it? And how was it?' Then my father asked him, 'where are you from?' The man said, 'from the people of Sham.' My father said, 'where do you live?' The man said, 'in Bayt al-Maqdis.'[3] My father said, 'have you read the two books?'[4] The man said, 'yes.'

"My father said, 'oh, brother of the northern [or sham] people, remember what I will say and narrate nothing but the truth of what you will hear. Regarding the beginning of this tawaf at this house, Allah said to the angels, "I am placing a successor on earth." The angels said, "oh Allah, a successor that is not one of us, who will corrupt and shed blood, and who will envy, hate, and assault each other? Oh please Allah, make that successor one of us. We will not cause corruption, shed blood, envy, hate, or assault each other, while we declare your praises, sanctify and obey you, and will never disobey you." Allah said, "I know what you do not know." So, the angels thought that what they said had made Allah angry, therefore they went to the Throne, raised their heads up and pointed with their fingers while making supplication with humiliation. They wept out of their fear of Allah, then they did tawaf around the Throne for three hours. Allah looked at them and his mercy descended upon them, then He placed a House underneath the Throne; it was based on four columns of peridot, and covered with a burning red corundum stone, and He named that House the House of Tombs [al-Bayt al-Dhuraah].[5] Then Allah said to the angels, "do tawaf around this House and leave the Throne." So, the angels started doing tawaf around the House and they stopped circumambulating around the Throne, and it was made easier for them. This House is the Populous House [al-Bayt al-Ma'mour, البيت المعمور][6] of which Allah has mentioned that seventy thousand angels visit every day and night and leave, never returning to it. <u>Thereafter, Allah</u> said to the angels, "build a house for me on earth that is exactly

3. Bayt al-Maqdis, the 'Holy House,' likely refers to Jerusalem: 31.775731° 35.235631°.
4. Which two books is unclear, but it may refer to the Torah and the Zabur (psalms).
5. *Dhuraah* often refers to notable sepulchres and grave structures. The use of this term for the Ka'ba suggests that it was surrounded by notable tombs. This description applies better to the city of Petra which has over 1000 notable monuments (mostly tombs) than it would to Mecca in modern Saudi Arabia.
6. The name al-Bayt al-Ma'mour, the Populous House, suggests that the House was surrounded by a large population or city.

like this one," and He ordered all His creation on earth to do tawaf around it, just like the angels' tawaf of the Frequented Housed.'

"The man said, 'oh, son of the prophet's daughter, you have told the truth, this is how it was.'"

> The word 'holy' was originally reserved for God. However, during the Christian epoch after the fifth century, the word holy developed a wider application and was used for great churches, tombs, and Christian civic buildings. The word Maqdis' appears in Qur'an 5:21, where Musa (Moses) tells the people to enter the Holy Land. 'Holy Land' only appears once in the Bible, Zechariah 2:12, which was written during the reign of Darius the Great, long after the time of Moses. The Qur'an refers to the spirit of God as holy four times (2:87; 2:253; 5:110; 16:102). Two centuries after Muḥammad, by the time of Ibn Ishaq and Azraqi, the term holy had expanded to include the Ka'ba, calendar months, holy ground, holy territories, holy cities, and holy war.

The Angels Visit the House
6 - Abu al-Walid narrated to us, saying, Mahdi ibn Abi al-Mahdi narrated to me, saying, Abdul Razzaq narrated to us, saying, Umar ibn Bakkar narrated to us, on the authority of Wahb ibn Munabbih, on the authority of Ibn Abbas:

"Jibril stood by prophet Muḥammad, and he (Jibril) was wearing a dusty red turban. The prophet said, 'oh, honest spirit, what is this dust on your turban?' He replied, "I visited the House, and the angels crowded around the Corner. This dust you see is caused by their fluttering wings.'

7 - And my grandfather informed me, on the authority of Sa'id ibn Salim, on the authority of Uthman ibn Saj, who said, Uthman ibn Yasar informed me, saying:

"I have heard—and Allah knows best—that if Allah wanted to send an angel for some affairs on earth, the angel would ask Allah's permission to do tawaf around the House. Then he descended quite pleased."

Similarly narrated by Wahb ibn Munabbih: "The angel prays two Raka'at in the House."

8 - And my grandfather informed me, on the authority of Sa'id ibn Salim, on the authority of Uthman ibn Saj, who said, 'Abbad ibn Kathir informed me, on the authority of Layth ibn Mu'adh, who said, the prophet said:

"This House is the fifth of fifteen houses. Seven of which are in the heavens up to the Throne, and seven to the frontiers of the lowest earth. The highest one is the one underneath the Throne, al-Bayt al-Ma'mour, and each one has a sanctuary [or haram] like the sanctuary of this House. If one house falls, they will all fall upon each other all the way to the frontiers of the lowest earth. Each house is frequented either by residents of the heavens or people of the earth, just like this House."

9 - Abu al-Walid narrated to us, saying, my grandfather narrated to me, on the authority of Sa'id ibn Salim, on the authority of Uthman, on the authority of Wahb ibn Munabbih, that Ibn Abbas informed him:

"Jibril stood by prophet Muḥammad and he (Jibril) was wearing a dusty green turban. The prophet said, 'oh, honest spirit, what is this dust on your turban?' He replied, 'I visited the House, and the angels crowded around the Corner. This dust you see is caused by their fluttering wings.'"

Adam's Forbidden House
10 - Abu al-Walid narrated to us, saying, my grandfather narrated to us, saying, Sa'id ibn Salim narrated to us, on the authority of Talhah ibn Amr al-Hadrami, on the authority of Atta' ibn Abi Rabah, on the authority of Ibn Abbas, who said:

"When Allah sent Adam down from Paradise to earth, his head was in the sky and his feet were on earth, and he was trembling like a boat on a rough sea. Then Allah decreased Adam's size to sixty cubits [or dhira'], and he said, 'oh Allah, why can't I hear the angels' sound, or feel their presence?' Allah said, 'oh Adam, it is because of your sin. But go and build me a house, and then do tawaf and praise and remember me around it, just as you have seen the angels doing around My Throne.'"

Then the narrator added: "Adam came on foot; the earth folded back at his tread, and he was able to cross a whole desert in one stride. He also crossed all stretches of water or seas in one step. Each place he crossed become prosperous and blessed, until he arrived at Mecca where he built the Forbidden House [al-Bayt al-Haram]. Then Jibril stroked his wing against the earth, and he uncovered a solid mass [the foundation] of the lowest earth, and other angels threw large stones in it. The stones were so large that one stone could not be moved even by thirty men. Then Adam built the House from [the stones of] five mountains in Lebanon: Toor Zita,[7] Toor Sinaa,[8] al-Judi,[9] and Hira,[10] until it finally emerged on the surface of earth."

Ibn Abbas said: "so the first to lay the foundation of the House, pray in it, and do tawaf around it, was Adam. He continued until Allah sent the flood, which was an angry punishment from Allah."

The narrator continued :"wherever the flood reached, the trace of Adam was gone, but the flood did not reach the land of Sind[11] and Hind [or India]. Then when Allah sent Ibrahim and Ismail, they built up the House's foundations and marked

---

7. Or the Mount of Olives: 31.777908° 35.245685°.
8. Toor Sinaa could refer to Mount Horeb (28.555948° 33.976048°), or Jebal al-Lawz (28.654107° 35.305831°).
9. Al-Judi is a mountain in Turkey: 37.370292° 42.496901°.
10. Hira is a mountain in Iraq: 31.977557° 44.393404°.
11. Sindh is in Pakistan: 25.890902° 68.521632°.

its borders. After that, it was built by the Quraysh, and it is exactly underneath al-Bayt al-Ma'mour. If the latter falls, it will fall upon the House."

> Al-Bayt al-Haram is often translated as the Sacred House, but the word *haram* literally means forbidden. For example, the haram is the part of the home used by women where men are forbidden to enter. Large stone markers were erected around the haram area of the Forbidden House to indicate to pilgrims that they were entering a special area where killing, even of animals or plants, was forbidden. In Petra there are over 20 large square rocks that indicate the entrances into the forbidden area. No such markers have been found in Mecca in modern Saudi Arabia to indicate the border of the forbidden area.

11 - He said, Abu al-Walid narrated to us, saying, Mahdi ibn Abi Mahdi narrated to us, saying, Ismail ibn Abdul Karim al-San'ani narrated to us, on the authority of Abdul Samad ibn Ma'qal, on the authority of Wahb ibn Munabbih:

"When Allah the Almighty pardoned Adam, He ordered him to walk to Mecca, and He folded the earth back at his tread and made him able to cross each desert in one step and cross each stretch of water or sea in one step. Every place that Adam crossed became prosperous and blessed all the way until he reached Mecca.

"Before that Adam was in great sadness and he wept abundantly because of his great calamity, so that even the angels were saddened by his sadness and wept for his weeping. Then Allah consoled him with a tent from the tents of Paradise, and He placed it in Mecca at the place of Ka'ba, before the existence of the Ka'ba. That tent was a precious stone from the precious stones of Paradise; in it there were three golden lanterns from the raw gold of Paradise and a burning light from the light of Paradise. The Corner descended with it and, in those days, it was a white precious stone from the outskirts of Paradise. It was a chair for Adam to sit on. That tent was guarded by angels, and they drove the inhabitants of earth (who were the jinn and devils) away from the tent. [Jinn and devils] are not allowed to look at anything that comes down from Paradise, because Paradise is guaranteed for whoever looks at it.

"The earth was immaculate and pure at that time. There was not any impurity, blood shedding, or wrongdoing, for Allah made earth a habitation for angels, and He made them glorify Allah day and night without tiring, as they did in heaven. They lined up in unity around the Haram; the lands outside the Haram [al-Hil] were behind them, and the Haram was in front of them. No jinn or devil could pass through them. Due to the superior status of the angels, Allah has made the Haram sacred to this day, and its borders are set on the place where the angels lined up.

"Allah the Almighty forbade Hawa [or Eve] from entering the Haram and looking at Adam's tent because of her sin that she committed in Paradise, so she did not look at anything there until Allah took her soul back. Whenever Adam wanted to meet Hawa he went outside the whole Haram. The tent remained in its place until Allah the Almighty took Adam's soul back, and then He raised it. The sons of Adam then built a house out of mud and stone in its place, and it continued to be occupied, generation after generation, until the time of Noah, when the House was inundated by the flood and its location disappeared.

"Then when Allah sent Ibrahim (friend of Allah), [Ibrahim] was looking for the foundation. When he arrived at the place, Allah the Almighty shaded it with a cloud, which marked the first House's borders. [The cloud] continued to be there and provided shade for Ibrahim. It guided him to the place of the foundation until Allah raised the foundation, and then the cloud left. Thus Allah's saying, '*we showed Ibrahim the location of the house*,' meaning the cloud that shaded the edges of the House to guide Ibrahim to the place of its foundation. Praise be to Allah, the House continued to be occupied since that time."

12 - Wahb ibn Munabbih said:
"I have read in one of the first books in which the Ka'ba was mentioned that every angel that Allah the Almighty has sent down to earth is ordered (by Allah) to visit the Ka'ba, so they swoop down from the Throne in a state of Ihram,[12] reciting the Talbiyah[13] until they touch the Corner, and then they do seven circuits of tawaf around the House, pray two Raka'at inside it, and they rise back to heaven."

13 - Muḥammad ibn Yahya narrated to me, on the authority of Ibrahim ibn Muḥammad ibn Abi Yahya, on the authority of Allah ibn Abi Labid, who said, it reached me that Ibn Abbas said:
"When Allah sent Adam to earth, he came down on the place of the Forbidden House. He was trembling like a boat in a rough sea, and then Allah sent the Black Stone down to him (the Corner), which was sparkling due to its extreme whiteness. Adam took the stone and squeezed it tightly in his arms, happy with it. Then Allah sent down the stick, and He ordered him, 'oh Adam, step over,' and he did, and found himself in the lands of Hind and Sind [or India]. Adam stayed there as long as Allah wanted him to stay, but then he started longing for the Corner, so he was told, 'perform Hajj [or pilgrimage],' and so he did. Then the angels met him and said to him, 'may Allah accept your Hajj; we did Hajj at this House two thousand years before you.'"

14 - My grandfather narrated to me, saying, Sa'id ibn Salim narrated to us, on the authority of Uthman ibn Saj, who said, Muḥammad ibn Ishaq informed me, saying:
"I have heard that when Adam was sent down to earth, he was saddened by being deprived of all the things that he used to see and hear, worshipping Allah in Paradise. Therefore, Allah granted him the Forbidden House and ordered him to walk

---
12. A state of consecration and preparation for pilgrimage.
13. A liturgical prayer offered by pilgrims during the pilgrimages.

to it, and wherever he encamped Allah made pure running water burst for him. This continued all the way until he reached Mecca where he settled, worshipping Allah, and doing tawaf around the House, and he kept doing that until he died there."

15 - My grandfather narrated to me, saying, Sa'id ibn Salim narrated to me on the authority of Uthman ibn Saj, who said:
"I have heard Umar ibn al-Khattab asking Ka'b, 'oh Ka'b, tell me about the Forbidden House.' Ka'b said, 'Allah the Almighty sent it down from Paradise as a hollowed precious stone with Adam, and told him, "oh Adam, this is My House, I sent it down with you. Tawaf will be done around it like the tawaf around My Throne, and prayers will be performed around it like the prayers around My Throne." Angels were sent down with it to raise its foundations out of stone, and then the House was put on these foundations. Adam did tawaf around it like the tawaf that is done around the Throne, and he performed prayers around it like the prayers that are performed around the Throne. When Allah drowned the people of Noah, He raised it to heaven and its foundations remained.'"

Abban ibn Abi Ayash said: "we have heard from the companions of Allah's prophet that Umar ibn al-Khattab asked Ka'b, and he narrated the same story."

16 - My grandfather narrated to me, saying, Ibrahim ibn Muḥammad ibn Abi Yahya narrated to me, on the authority of al-Zuhri, on the authority of Ubayd Allah ibn Abdullah ibn Utbah ibn Mas'ud, on the authority of Ibn Abbas, who said:
"The first to place foundations and to pray at the House was Adam, until Allah sent the flood."

17 - Mahdi ibn Abi al-Mahdi narrated to us, saying, Abdullah ibn Ma'adh al-San'ani narrated to us, on the authority of Ma'mar, on the authority of Abban:
"The House was sent down as a precious stone, or one pearl, for Adam."

18 - My grandfather narrated to me, saying, Sa'id ibn Salim al-Qaddah narrated to us, on the authority of Uthman ibn Saj, on the authority of Wahb ibn Munabbih, who said:
"The House that Allah gave to Adam was a precious stone from the precious stones of Paradise. It was burning red. It had two doors, one faced east, and the other faced west. It had lanterns to light—gold vessels from the raw gold of Paradise, and they were decorated with white stars. The Corner at that time was a star from the stars, and it was a white precious stone."

> The 19th-century English scholar and poet John Burgon famously described Petra as "a rose-red city half as old as time." He was not the first to exaggerate the beautiful red sandstone of the Petra area, also known as the Seir mountains. Al-Azraqi recounts several descriptions of the first House of Islam as a burning red ruby (or precious stone). Today there is nothing about the Ka'ba building in Mecca to make us think of the color red. But the original Ka'ba in Petra was built from red sandstone, like much of the rest of the city.

19 - My grandfather narrated to us, saying, Ibrahim ibn Muḥammad ibn Abi Yahya narrated to me, saying, al-Mughira ibn Ziyad narrated to us, on the authority of Atta' ibn Abi Rabah, who said:
"When Ibn al-Zubayr was building the Ka'ba, he asked the workers to dig deep into the ground. They reached rocks that looked like pregnant camels."[14]

He continued: "the workers then said, 'we have reached giant rocks that look like pregnant camels.' Ibn al-Zubayr said, 'dig deeper,' and when they did, they faced an appearance of fire. He said, 'what has happened?' They said, 'we cannot dig further; we have seen a great thing and we cannot continue.' Ibn al-Zubayr said, 'build on top of it.'"

The narrator said: "they believed that the rock was from Adam's building."

20 - My grandfather narrated to me, on the authority of Sa'id ibn Salim, on the authority of Uthman ibn Saj, on the authority of al-Zuhri, on the authority of Ubayd Allah ibn Utbah, on the authority of Ibn Abbas:
"Adam prostrated while he was weeping. Then a voice called out to him, 'oh Adam, why are you weeping?' He said, 'I am weeping because of the obstruction between me and your angels' glorification, and between me and the sanctification of your sanctuary.' He was told, 'oh Adam, go to the Forbidden House.' So, he went out to Mecca, and each place where he stepped pure water burst forth, and prosperous settlement and cities arose, while ruins and deserts were between his feet.

"I have heard that Adam wept when he remembered Paradise. If Adam's weeping when he was exiled from Paradise is compared to the weeping of all the creatures, [his weeping] would exceed it. And if the weeping of Dawud[15] when he sinned is compared to the weeping of all the creatures, together with the weeping of Adam, it would exceed it."

21 - My grandfather narrated to me, saying, Sa'id ibn Salim informed us, on the authority of Uthman ibn Saj, on the authority of Wahb ibn Munabbih:
"Adam wept abundantly and was greatly saddened because of his calamity. The angels were saddened by his sadness and wept for his weeping."

---
14. Rocks like "pregnant camels" probably means large rocks.
15. The Muslim parallel of the Biblical King David.

The narrator continued: "then Allah the Almighty consoled him with a tent from the tents of Paradise. He placed it in Mecca, at the place of the Ka'ba, before the existence of the Ka'ba. The tent was a precious stone from the precious stones of Paradise; in it there were three golden lanterns from the raw gold of Paradise and a burning light from the light of Paradise. That tent was guarded by angels, and they drove the inhabitants of the earth (who were the jinn and devils) away from the tent. [Jinn and devils] are not allowed to look at anything that comes down from Paradise, because Paradise is guaranteed for whoever looks at it.

"The earth was immaculate and pure at that time. There was not any impurity, blood shedding, or wrongdoing. For this reason, Allah made earth a habitation for angels and He made them glorify Allah day and night without tiring, as they did in heaven. The tent remained in its place until Allah the Almighty took Adam's soul back, and then He raised it."

22 - Mahdi ibn Abi al-Mahdi narrated to me, on the authority of Abdullah ibn Ma'adh al-San'ani, on the authority of Ma'mar, on the authority of Qatta'dah, regarding the saying of the Almighty, "we showed Ibrahim the location of the House," he said:

"Allah the Almighty sent down the House with Adam. When Adam descended to the earth, he landed on the land of Hind [or India]. Adam's head was in the sky while his feet were on earth. At that time the angels feared him. Then Allah the Almighty decreased [Adam's] height to sixty cubits [or dhira']. Adam was saddened because he could no longer hear the voices of the angels glorifying Allah, so he complained to Allah. Then Allah the Almighty told him, 'oh Adam, I sent down a House with you. Tawaf will be done around it like the tawaf around My Throne, so go to that House.' Adam set off, and Allah extended his steps. In every two steps he crossed a whole desert. He continued like that until he reached the House. Adam did tawaf around the House, and so did the prophets after him.

23 - Muḥammad ibn Yahya narrated to me, on the authority of Abdul Aziz ibn Imran, on the authority of Umar ibn Abi Ma'ruf, on the authority of Abdullah ibn Abi Ziyad, who said:

"When Allah the Almighty sent Adam down from Paradise, He (Allah) said, 'oh Adam, build me a House corresponding (or similar) to my House in the sky. You and your children will worship me in it, just as angels are worshipping me around My Throne.' The angels descended to [Adam], and he dug down to the seventh earth. The angels threw large stones in it until it was level with the earth's surface. A hollowed red precious stone that had four white corners descended to Adam, and he put it on top of the foundation. The precious stone stayed there until the flood, when Allah the Almighty raised it."

The Supplication of Adam's Offspring and Tawaf Recitations

24 - He said, Abu al-Walid narrated to us, saying, my grandfather narrated to me, on the authority of Sa'id ibn Salim, on the authority of Uthman ibn Saj, who said:

"I have been told that Adam went out to Mecca and he built the House. When he finished building, he said, 'my Lord, every servant has a reward, and I have a reward!' Allah said, 'yes, ask Me.' Adam said, 'oh Allah, return me to the place where You had taken me out.' Allah said, 'yes, you will get what you hoped for.' Adam said, 'and any one of my offspring who comes to this House, acknowledging their sins like I did, forgive them.' Allah said, 'yes, you will get what you hoped for.'"

25 - He said, Abu al-Walid narrated to us, saying, Muḥammad ibn Yahya narrated to us, on the authority of Ibrahim ibn Muḥammad ibn Abi Yahya, on the authority of Abu al-Malih who said, Abu-Huraira used to say:

"Adam performed Hajj and he completed all the rituals. When he was done, he said, 'oh Allah, every servant has a reward.' Allah the Almighty said, 'I have forgiven you, and those of your offspring who will come to this House and acknowledge their sins and ask forgiveness, they shall be forgiven.' Then Adam performed Hajj, and the angels came to him at al-Radm and said to him, 'may Allah accept your Hajj. We did Hajj at this House two thousand years before you.' Adam asked, 'what did you say around it?' The angels answered, 'we used to say, "subhan Allah" [glory be to Allah], "Alhamdulillah" [praise be to Allah], "la ilaha illa Allah" [there is no god except Allah], and "Allahu akbar" [Allah is the greatest].' Therefore, whenever Adam did tawaf around the House, he said these words. Adam's tawaf was seven weeks at night, and five weeks at daytime.'"

Nafi' said: "Ibn Umar used to do that."

> Al-Radm, where the angels visited Adam, was a levee built to prevent flood waters from reaching the Ka'ba. This feature is found in Petra; the *radm* or dam at the entrance of the siq slowly eroded away until flash floods in 1963 killed 22 French tourists and a local guide. A modern dam was built at the same place as the original dam so that flood waters could be diverted north through an ancient tunnel, around Petra. No such ancient dam exists in Mecca in modern Saudi Arabia.

26 - Muḥammad ibn Yahya narrated to me, saying, Hisham ibn Sulayman al-Makhzumi narrated to me, on the authority of Abdullah ibn Abi Sulayman, the freedman of Banu Makhzum, who said:

"Adam did tawaf (seven times) around the House when he descended. Then he prayed two Raka'at in front of the Ka'ba's door, after which he went to al-Multazim and said, 'oh Allah, You know my secret and my revelation; accept my excuse. You know what I have done, so forgive my sins. You know my needs, so give me what I ask, oh Allah. I ask You for a faith that fills my heart, and a sincere certainty until I know that nothing will happen to me except what You have ordained for me, and contentment with what You have judged me.' Allah revealed to him, 'oh Adam, I have answered the supplication with which you called to me, and any one of your offspring who will call on me with this supplication, I will have his distress and worries removed, his confusion stopped, and I will take poverty out of his heart, and I will make him benefit from the trade of every trader, and his worldly gains will undoubtedly come to him, even if he does not want them.'"

The narrator continued: "since the tawaf of Adam, the sunnah of tawaf started."

27 - Muḥammad ibn Yahya narrated to me, saying, Hisham ibn Sulayman al-Makhzumi narrated to me, on the authority of Abdullah ibn Abi Sulayman, the freedman of Banu Makhzum, who said:
"The first thing that Adam did when he descended from the sky was the tawaf around the House, and then the angels came to him and they said, 'may Allah accept your rituals; we did Hajj at this House two thousand years before you.'"

28 - My grandfather narrated to me, on the authority of Sufyan ibn Uyaynah, on the authority of al-Haram ibn Abi Labid al-Madani, who said:
"Adam performed Hajj; then the angels met him and they said, 'oh Adam, may Allah accept your Hajj; we did Hajj two thousand years before you.'"

29 - My grandfather narrated to me, on the authority of Sa'id ibn Salim, on the authority of Uthman ibn Saj, who said:
"I was told by Sa'id that Adam [performed the] Hajj 70 times, and that the angels met him between al-Ma'zimain[16] and they told him, 'oh Adam, may Allah accept your Hajj; we did Hajj two thousand years before you.'"

30 - My grandfather narrated to me, on the authority of Sa'id ibn Salim, on the authority of Talhah, on the authority of Atta' ibn Amr al-Hadrami, on the authority of Ibn Abi Rabah, on the authority of Ibn Abbas, who said:
"Adam performed Hajj, and he did tawaf (seven rounds) around the House. The angels met him there and said, 'oh Adam, may Allah accept your Hajj; we did Hajj two thousand years before you.' Adam asked, 'what did you say while doing tawaf?' The angels answered, 'we used to say, "subhan Allah [glory be to Allah], and "al-hamdulillah" [praise be to Allah], and "la ilaha illa Allah' [there is no god except Allah], and "Allahu akhbar" [Allah is the greatest].' Adam said, 'add to these "la hawla wala quwwata illa billah" [there is no might nor strength except with Allah].'"

The narrator said: "the angels added this. Then Ibrahim performed Hajj after he built the House, and the angels met him while he was doing tawaf and they greeted him. Ibrahim asked them, 'what did you say while doing tawaf?' They said, 'before your father Adam we used to say, "subhan Allah," "alhamdulillah," "la ilaha illa Allah," and "Allahu akhbar." Then we told Adam these words and he asked us

---

16. Al-Ma'zimain is mentioned in the *'Ittaba al-Sunnah:* "the Imam set off on the return from 'Arafat; we also returned with him until we reached the narrow path which is before al-Ma'zimain." This passage suggests al-Ma'zimain is located near the base of 'Arafat Mountain. *Bibliotheca Indica Vol 1.* describes it as the boundary of the Haram area at the base of 'Arafat Mountain. Dan Gibson locates it at: 30.314654° 35.428526°.

to add "la hawla wala quwwata illa billah."' Ibrahim said, 'and add to it "al-Aliu al-Adeem" [the Most High, the Magnificent].'"

The narrator reported: "so the angels did that."

Allah Proclaims His Greatness to Adam

31 - Abu al-Walid narrated to us, saying, my grandfather narrated to me, on the authority of Sa'id ibn Salim, on the authority of Uthman ibn Saj, on the authority of Wahb ibn Munabbih, who said: "When Adam descended to the earth, he felt lonely in the vast space of the earth where there was no one apart from him on it, so he said, 'my Lord, does this earth of Yours have only me to live on it and to praise and sanctify You?' Allah said, 'I shall have some of your offspring praise and sanctify me, and I shall have houses raised [on the earth] so that My creatures may proclaim My name and praise Me, and I shall grant you one house I choose for Myself, and I will favor it with my dignity, and distinguish it from all other houses by My Name and call it My House. I shall have it proclaimed by My Greatness, and it is upon it that I have placed My sacredness, and I shall make it the worthiest of houses in which My name should be mentioned, and I shall locate it in a spot I choose for Myself. Therefore, I chose its place the day I created the heavens and the earth, and before that it was my volition, as it is my chosen House. I do not live in it, and I should not live in houses, as they cannot contain Me, but on the chair of pride and might, which is distinguished by My majesty, upon it I have placed My greatness and My glory and settled My stability. However, it is powerless without My power. Then I, filling everything, and being above everything, and together with everything, and surrounding everything, and in front of everything, and behind everything, nothing could know My knowledge, nor be capable to perform My power, nor reach My status—I shall make that House for you and for those after you a sanctuary and a safe place; its sacredness will extend to everything above it, underneath it, and around it. Those who make it sacred, they have greatened My sacredness, and those who ignore it, they have violated My sacredness. Whoever seeks the safety of its people deserve My safety, and whoever frightens them forfeits My protection. Whoever glorifies its status becomes great in My eyes, and whoever neglects it becomes lowly in My eyes. Every king has possession of what is around it, and [the people of] the valley of Mecca are My finest, and My Possession, and the neighbors of My house, and its builders and its visitors, and they shall be granted My hospitality and My protection by My side.

"'Then I shall make it the first House established for mankind, and I shall frequent it with the residence of heaven and the people of earth. They will come to it in groups, disheveled and covered with dust on every transport available, and they will come from every distant point shouting emotionally, "Allah akhbar; la ilaha illa Allah," and shedding abundant tears. For those who visit the House for My sake only, they have visited Me and came to Me, and whoever comes to Me I shall bless with My dignity, as it is the duty of the generous to honor his guests and give them what they need. Oh Adam, you shall dwell there as long as you live; then after you the nations shall swell there, the generations and the prophets, one nation after the other, one generation after the other, and one prophet after the other. It will be like that until [the generations] reach a prophet from your offspring.

"'He is the last of prophets. I shall make him of those who maintain the House, and those who dwell in it, protect it, rule it, and give water to its pilgrims. I shall make him a guardian of the House as long as he lives, and when he comes back to Me, he will find what I have reserved for him as his reward. [His] virtue will allow Him to come near Me and be granted the highest place [al-Waseela], and the most superior place in Paradise.

"'And I shall make the name of that house, its mention, its honor, its glory, and its praise, belong to a prophet, descended from your son, who will be before this prophet. His Father is called Ibrahim. I shall raise the foundations of the House for him, and make him build it and maintain it, and give him the task of giving water to its pilgrims, and show him what is allowed and what is forbidden in it, and teach him its rituals, and make him one nation. His complete obedience is to Me, performing My commands, and guiding people to My way. I shall choose him and guide him to a straight path. I shall afflict Him (with calamities) and he will be patient. I shall keep him safe, and he will thank Me. He will make vows to Me and fulfill them. He will promise Me and keep his promise. I shall answer the prayers of his children and offspring after him, and I shall make him intercessor to them.

"'Then I shall make them the people of that House, and its rulers, its protectors, its servants, and its pilgrims, until they start changing [these things] and making innovations [bida'ah, بدع]. If they start doing that, and then I, Allah the most capable, can replace them with other people. I shall make Ibrahim the leader [or imam] of the people of that House and the people of Islamic law [sharia'a]. He will lead everyone who comes to this place, human beings and jinn; they will follow his sunnah and be guided by his good deeds.

"'So those who have [followed him], they have fulfilled their promise and completed their rituals. And those who have not done that, they have wasted their rituals and lost their goal. If anyone asks where I am on that day, I am with those who are disheveled and covered with dust, who fulfilled their promises and completed their rituals—those who pray to their God, the ones who know what they reveal and what they conceal. Not this creation, nor this matter that I have narrated to you, Adam, would increase a thing in My sovereignty, or My greatness, or My power and authority, or My possessions any more than a drop of a splash of water which falls in seven seas linked to another seven seas, countless. Yet, the drop of water adds to the sea more than this creation matter would add to what I have. And if I did not create this, it would not diminish a thing of My kingdom, or My greatness, or of what I have of wealth and abundance, any more than a mote which falls from the earth's soil, mountains, grit, sand, and trees. Yet, the mote can decrease something of earth's soil more than this creation matter would to what I have if I did not create it.' This is an example of the power of the Almighty, the Wise."

A similar account was narrated by Wahb ibn Munabbih.

Seventy Thousand Angels Visit al-Bayt al-Ma'mour which is Ad-Dhuraah

32 - Abu al-Walid narrated to us, saying, my grandfather narrated to me, saying, Sa'id ibn Salim narrated to me, on the authority of Uthman ibn Saj, on the authority of Wahb ibn Munabbih, who said, Abu Sa'id informed me, on the authority of Muqatil, raising the narration to the prophet in a hadith he narrated, saying, I was told by Abu Sa'id, regarding Muqatil, who was telling a hadith of the prophet Muḥammad, and said:

"It was named al-Bayt al-Ma'mour[17] [the Populous House] because every day seventy thousand angels pray in that House; then at evening they descend to the Ka'ba and do tawaf around it, and then they greet the prophet and leave. No calamity befalls them until the Last Hour [or the resurrection] comes.'"

33 - My grandfather narrated to me, on the authority of Sa'id ibn Salim, on the authority of Uthman ibn Saj, on the authority of Wahb ibn Munabbih:

"it is (mentioned) in the Torah—a House in the sky opposite to the Ka'ba, above its dome. It is called Ad-Dhuraah.[18] This is al-Bayt al-Ma'mour; it is visited by seventy thousand angels every day, and they never come back to it."

34 - My grandfather narrated to me, on the authority of Sa'id ibn Salim, who said, Ibn Jurayj informed me, on the authority of Safwan ibn Sulaym, on the authority of Kurayb, the freedman of Ibn Abbas, on the authority of Ibn Abbas, who said, the prophet said:

"The House in the sky is called Ad-Dhuraah and it is built in the same way as this Forbidden House. If it (the one in the sky) falls, it will fall upon it. Every day it is visited by seventy thousand angels, and they never come back to it."

35 - My grandfather narrated to me, on the authority of Sa'id ibn Salim, on the authority of Uthman ibn Saj, who said, Muḥammad ibn al-Sa'ib al-Kalbi said:

"I have heard, and Allah knows best, that a house in the sky called Ad-Dhuraah, opposite to the Ka'ba, is visited by seventy thousand angels every day, who have never visited it before."

36 - My grandfather narrated to me, saying, Sufyan ibn Uyaynah narrated to me, on the authority of Ibn Abi Husayn, on the authority of Abu al-Tufayl, who said:

"Ibn al-Kowaa' asked Ali, 'what is al-Bayt al-Ma'mour?' Ali said, 'it is Ad-Dhuraah, and it is near (or opposite) to this House, and it is in the sixth sky. Every day seventy thousand angels enter it; they never come back to it.'"

---

17. While Muqatil attributes the name "the Populous House" to the vast numbers of angels who visit the Ka'ba in the sky daily, the historical Ka'ba may have simply earned that name by being surrounded by a city.

18. Dhuraah, الضراح, often refers to notable sepulchres and grave structures. The use of this term for the al-Bayt al-Ma'mour may suggest that the historical Ka'ba was surrounded by notable tombs.

Sufyan ibn Uyana narrated a similar account, but he said: "in the seventh sky," and also said, "they never come back to it until the Day of Judgement."

37 - Abu al-Walid narrated to us, saying, Mahdi ibn Abi al-Mahdi narrated to us, saying, Abdullah ibn Ma'adh al-San'ani narrated to us, saying, Ma'mar narrated to us, on the authority of Wahb ibn Abdullah, on the authority of Abu al-Tufayl, who said:

"I have witnessed Ali delivering a speech and he said, 'ask me. By Allah, anything you ask me about that exists until the Day of Judgement, I will tell you about it. And ask me about the Book of Allah [or the Qur'an]. By Allah, there is no verse [ayah] in it [of which I do not] know whether it was revealed at night or at daytime, or if it was revealed on flat ground or on a mountain.' Then Ibn al-Kowaa' stood up (he was behind me and I was between him and Ali), and he said: 'do you know about al-Bayt al-Ma'mour? What is it?' Ali said, 'it is Ad-Dhuraah, above seven skies, underneath the Throne. Every day seventy thousand angels enter it, and they never come back to it until the Day of Judgement.'"

Al-Bayt al-Ma'mour's Removal at the Time of the Flood

38 - Abu al-Walid narrated to us, saying, my grandfather narrated to me, saying, Sa'id ibn Salim narrated to us, on the authority of Ibn Jurayj, on the authority of Mujahid, who said:

"I have heard that when Allah the Almighty created the heavens and the earth, the first thing He placed on it was the Forbidden House. At that time, it was a hollowed red precious stone with two doors; one was eastern and the other was western. Allah placed it opposite to al-Bayt al-Ma'mour, until the time of the flood, when it (the House) was raised up by two pieces of silk [dibaj]. It will remain there until the Day of Judgement. Allah the Almighty entrusted the Corner to Aba Kobais."[19]

The narrator continued: "and Ibn Abbas said, 'it was gold, and it was raised up at the time of the flood, so it is in the sky.'"

39 - And Ibn Jurayj said, Juwaybir said:

"Al-Bayt al-Ma'mour was in Mecca; it was raised up at the time of flood, so it is in the sky.'"

40 - My grandfather narrated to me, on the authority of Sa'id ibn Salim, on the authority of Uthman ibn Saj, who said, Abu Sa'id informed me, on the authority of Muqatil, raising the narration to the prophet, in a hadith he narrated, that Adam said:

"'Oh God, I know my misfortune; I cannot see any of Your light being worshipped.' Therefore, Allah the Almighty sent down al-Bayt al-Ma'mour to him. It was as wide as this House in its place, a red precious stone, but its height was [equal to] what is between the sky and the earth. And He, Allah, ordered Adam to do tawaf around it. Allah then removed his sorrows that he felt previously. After that, the House was raised at the time of Noah.'"

---

19. أبا قبيس, a mountain in Mecca.

The Forbidden House Built by the Sons of Adam

41 - Abu al-Walid narrated to us, saying, my grandfather narrated to us, on the authority of Sa'id ibn Salim, on the authority of Uthman ibn Saj, on the authority of Wahb ibn Munabbih, who said:

"when the tent was raised, which Allah the Almighty had sent to Adam from the jewels of Paradise to the place of the House in Mecca to relieve his pain, the sons of Adam built a house out of mud and stones in its place after Adam's death. The House was frequented by them and those who came after them until the time of Noah, when it was demolished by the flood which changed its place. Then its place was shown to Ibrahim."

Noah's Ark Circumambulates the House

42 - Abu al-Walid narrated to us, saying, Mahdi ibn Abi al-Mahdi narrated to us, saying, Bishr ibn al-Sari al-Basri narrated to us, on the authority of Dawud ibn Abi al-Furat al-Kindi, on the authority of Albaa ibn Ahmar al-Yashkari, on the authority of Ikrimah, on the authority of Ibn Abbas, who said:

"there were 80 people with their families accompanying Noah in the ark. They stayed for a hundred and fifty days in the ark; then Allah directed them to Mecca, where the ark circumambulated the House for 40 days, and after that Allah directed it to mount al-Judi.[20]"

The narrator continued: "it landed there; then Noah sent out a raven to scout the earth, but it went eating and resting upon corpses and it did not return. Then Noah sent out a dove which came back holding an olive branch, and her legs were smeared with mud. Noah then knew the water had dried up, so he went down to the bottom of al-Judi, and he built a town and called it Thamaneen.[21] The people of Thamaneen woke up one day speaking 80 different languages; one of them is Arabic."

The narrator continued: "they did not understand each other, so Noah explained the meanings to them."

Allah Shows Ibrahim the Position of the Ka'ba

43 - Abu al-Walid narrated to us, saying, my grandfather narrated to me, on the authority of Sa'id ibn Salim, on the authority of Ibn Jurayj, on the authority of Mujahid, who said:

"The position of Ka'ba disappeared at the time of the flood, between Noah and Ibrahim."

The narrator said: "its position was a red hill of dry mud; floods cannot reach it. People knew that this was the place of the House, but its exact position is not confirmed. The place used to be visited by those who were oppressed and those who seek refuge from all parts of the earth, and distressed people used to supplicate there. Allah answered anyone who supplicated there. People used to go for pilgrimage to the place of the House until Allah showed Ibrahim its position when

---

20. Al-Judi is a mountain in Turkey: 37.370292° 42.496901°.
21. Thamaneen, ثمانين, literally means 80. The location of Thamaneen is unknown, but it is likely the Muslim parallel of Babel, the 80 referring to 80 different languages.

He, Allah, wanted His House to be built, and His religion and sacred law [sharia'a] to be revealed. The House has been sacred since the time Allah the Almighty sent Adam down to earth, and it will continue to be sacred and revered by the following nations and sects, one nation after the other, and one sect after the other."

He continued: "the angels used to perform pilgrimage at it before Adam."

Ibrahim Chooses the Location of the Ka'ba on Earth

44 - Abu al-Walid narrated to us, saying, my grandfather narrated to me, on the authority of Sa'id ibn Salim, on the authority of Ibn Saj, who said:

"I have heard (and Allah knows best) that Ibrahim Khalil[22] Allah ascended to heaven. He looked at the eastern parts and the western parts of the earth, and then he chose the place of the Ka'ba. The angels said to him: 'oh Khalil Allah, you chose Allah's sacred place on earth.'"

The narrator continued: "then he built it with stones from seven mountains."

He said: "and some say five mountains, and the angels brought the stones to Ibrahim from those mountains."

---

22. Khalil, خليل, means devoted friend. Ibrahim is commonly called Khalil Allah, or the devoted friend of Allah.

Chapter Two

Jibril Reveals Zamzam and the Forbidden House to Hajar

45 - Abu al-Walid narrated to us, saying, my grandfather narrated to me, saying, Sa'id ibn Salim narrated to me, on the authority of Uthman ibn Saj, who said, Muhammad ibn Ishaq informed me, saying, Ibn Abi Najih narrated to us, on the authority of Mujahid:

"when Allah the Almighty had shown the place of the House to Ibrahim, he came to it from al-Sham [North, or Syria and Palestine] along with his son Ismail, and Ismail's mother Hajar.[23] Ismail was at that time a suckling baby,[24] and they were transported by al-Buraq [البراق], as I have heard."

46 - Uthman ibn Saj narrated to us, on the authority of al-Hassan al-Basri, that he used to say, regarding the description of al-Buraq, that the prophet said:

"Jibril came to me with an animal, smaller than a mule and larger than a donkey, with two wings attached to its thighs, and prompted it to move. Its hoof reached to where the eye can reach."

Uthman said, Muhammad ibn Ishaq said: "Jibril was with prophet Ibrahim. He was showing him the place of the House and the features of the sanctuary."

The narrator continued: "they went out together. Whenever they passed a village, Ibrahim said, 'oh Jibril, is this what I have been commanded?' Jibril said, 'proceed.' [They traveled] until they reached Mecca, which at that time was full of thorny trees and inhabited by people called Amalek[25] who lived around Mecca. The House was at that time a red hill of dry mud. Ibrahim said to Jibril, 'is this where I have been commanded to put them?' Jibril said, 'yes.'"

The narrator continued: "Ibrahim took them to the place of the rock and placed them there. He ordered Hajar, Ismail's mother, to settle there and make the place shady. Then he said the verse, *'our Lord! Verily I have settled some of my progeny in a valley without cultivation'* (Qur'an 14:37). Ibrahim then went back to al-Sham and left them at the Forbidden House."

47 - My grandfather narrated to me, saying, Muslim ibn Khalid al-Zanji narrated to us, on the authority of Ibn Jurayj, on the authority of Kathir ibn Kathir ibn al-Muttalib ibn Abi Wada'ah al-Sahmi, on the authority of Sa'id ibn Jubayr, who said, Abdullah ibn Abbas narrated to us:

"After what happened between the mother of Ismail ibn Ibrahim and Sara, the wife of Ibrahim, Ibrahim brought Ismail who was a suckling baby and his mother to Mecca. Ismail's mother had a waterskin with her; she was drinking from it and breastfeeding her baby—she did not have any food with her."

---

23. Hajar is the parallel of Hagar in the Torah.
24. Ishmael was weaned when he and his mother were banished by Avraham in the Torah.
25. Amalekites, العماليق, descendants of Edom.

Sa'id ibn Jubayr continued, Ibn Abbas said: "and he (Ibrahim) brought them to a great tree above Zamzam, on top of the Mosque, pointing to the place between the well and al-Safa, and placed them underneath it. Then he went out riding his animal. Ismail's mother chased him until he reached a very poor land."

Ibn Abbas said: 'then Ismail's mother said to him (referring to herself), 'to whom are you leaving her and her child?'[26] Ibrahim said, 'to Allah the Almighty.' She said, 'I am content with Allah.' Then she went back, holding her child, and sat down underneath the great tree, placing her child next to her. She was drinking from her waterskin and feeding her baby until she ran out of water and could not produce more milk for her baby. He became hungry. Then his hunger became severe. His mother watched him become stiff and tense."

The narrator continued: "Ismail's mother thought he was dying, and that made her very sad."

Ibn Abbas said: "Ismail's mother said, 'if only I can go away so I would not see him dying.'"

Ibn Abbas said: "she went to al-Safa, as it was higher than the rest of the place, to see if there was anyone coming into the valley. Then she looked at al-Marwa and said, 'I will walk between these two mountains to be busy until the baby dies, so I will not watch him die.'"

Ibn Abbas said: "Ismail's mother walked between the two mountains three or four times, jogging when she was at the bottom of the valley."

Ibn Abbas said: "then Ismail's mother came back to her baby and found him still crying hard, as he was when she left him, and that made her very sad. She went again to al-Safa as an excuse so she would not see him dying, and she walked between the two mountains as she did the first time."

Ibn Abbas said: "until she walked seven times between them."

Ibn Abbas said, the prophet Abu al-Qasim[27] said: "for that reason people walk between al-Safa and al-Marwa."

Ibn Abbas continued: "then she came back to her child and found him still crying. Then she heard a voice coming towards them; no one was with her. She said, 'I can hear your voice; help me if you have something good with you.'"

The narrator said: "then Jibril appeared to her, and she followed him. He kicked the ground with his foot at the place of the well, referring to Zamzam. Then water flowed on top of the ground at the place where Jibril kicked."

Ibn Abbas said, Abu al-Qasim said: "Ismail's mother started forming the soil as a basin around the water, so it would not fade away before she brought her waterskin. She filled her waterskin with water and drank from it, and then she breastfed her child."

---

26. Ismail's mother, Hajar, here refers to herself in the third person.
27. Muḥammad.

48 - My grandfather narrated to me, saying, Sa'id ibn Salim narrated to us, on the authority of Uthman ibn Saj, who said, Muḥammad ibn Ishaq said:

"I have been told that an angel came to Hajar, Ismail's mother, when Ibrahim left her in Mecca, before the raising of the foundations of the House by Ibrahim and Ismail. The angel pointed to the House, which was at that time a red hill of dry mud, and said to her, 'this is the first House established for mankind on earth, and it is the Ancient House of Allah. It will be built by Ibrahim and Ismail.'"

Ibn Jarih said: "I have been told that when Jibril dug into the place of Zamzam with his heel, he pointed to the place of the House and said to Ismail's mother, 'this is the first House established for mankind, for this is the ancient House of Allah which will be built by Ibrahim and Ismail for mankind. They will frequent it, and it will be frequented, sacred, and honored until the Day of Judgement.'"

Ibn Jarih said: "Ismail's mother died before Ibrahim and Ismail built the House, and she was buried at the place of the stone.[28]"

49 - My grandfather narrated to me, on the authority of Sa'id ibn Salim, on the authority of Uthman ibn Saj, who said, Ali ibn Abdullah ibn al-Wazi' informed me, on the authority of Ayyub al-Sakhtiyani, on the authority of Sa'id ibn Jubayr, on the authority of Ibn Abbas:

"The angel who [revealed] Zamzam to Hajar said to her, 'the father of this boy will come and build a house at this spot,' and he pointed at the place of the House. Then the angel set off."

The Arrival of the Jurhum and the Selection of Ismail's Wife

50 - My grandfather narrated to me, on the authority of Muslim ibn Khalid al-Zanji, on the authority of Ibn Jurayj, on the authority of Kathir ibn Kathir, on the authority of Sa'id ibn Jubayr, on the authority of Ibn Abbas, who said:

"Not a long time after Allah the Almighty drew the water of Zamzam out for Ismail's mother, a caravan of the tribe of Jurhum[29] passed by while they were coming from al-Sham, through the bottom of the valley. They saw some birds flying above the place of the water. They said, 'this valley is not a place of water or inhabitants.'"

Ibn Abbas said: "they sent two messengers towards the place. When those messengers found Ismail's mother, they talked with her. Then they went back to their caravan and reported where she was."

The narrator continued: "the whole caravan headed to her place. They greeted her and she answered them. They asked, 'whose water is this?' Ismail's mother replied, 'it is mine.' They asked, 'will you allow us to stay with you [near the water]?' She said, 'yes'"

Ibn Abbas said, Abu al-Qasim said: "Ismail's mother was pleased, as she used to enjoy the company of people. They settled there and sent for their families who came later. [The Jurhum] settled in with them under the great trees which made

---

28. The place of the stone, al-Hijr, was known later as the Stone of Ismail.
29. The Jurhum, جرهم, known in Greek as the Geramenoi, were an Arab tribe which controlled Mecca and the Ka'ba prior to the Quraysh.

it a shady residence for them. And she (Ismail's mother) and her child lived with them until [Ismail] grew up; they admired Ismail while he was growing up amongst them. Later on, Ismail's mother died. The Jurhum lived by hunting and Ismail learned [to hunt] from them. They used to go with Ismail outside the Sanctuary to hunt. When Ismail reached the age of puberty they made him marry a woman from them."

The narrator continued: "she was mentioned in the al-Mubtada'[30] book."

Ubayd ibn Salamah said, Muḥammad ibn Ishaq said: "the name of Ismail's wife was Umara bint Sa'id ibn Osama."

Ibn Abbas said: "Ibrahim came from al-Sham, as he said, 'to see my dependents I left in Mecca.' When he arrived in Mecca, he found Ismail's wife and asked her about Ismail. She said, 'he is not here.' She did not speak nicely to him, so Ibrahim said to her, 'when Ismail comes back tell him, "a sheikh came after you had left and he sends you his greetings and tells you to change the threshold of your house, as I did not approve it."'"

Ibn Abbas said: "each time Ismail came back to his home he used to ask his wife, 'has anyone come after I left?' So, when he asked, his wife said, 'a sheikh came,' and she described him. Ismail asked, 'did you say anything to him?' She said, 'no.' Then Ismail asked, 'did he tell you anything?' She said, 'yes, he sends his greetings and tells you to change the threshold of your house, as he did not approve it.' Ismail said, 'you are the threshold of my house, so go to your family.' Ismail divorced her and they (the Jurhum) made him marry another woman."

Ibn Abbas said: "Ibrahim stayed away for some time and then he came back to visit Ismail. Again, he did not find him, but he found his new wife. Ibrahim greeted her. She greeted him back and asked him to stay for some time with them and to have something to eat and drink. Ibrahim asked, 'what is your food and drink?' She replied, 'meat and water.' He said, 'do you have grains or any other food?' She said, 'no.' Ibrahim said, 'may Allah bless your food and your drink.'"

Ibn Abbas said, "the prophet said, 'if on that day he (Ibrahim) had found any grains in Ismail's house, he would have prayed to Allah to bless their grains, and that land would have become a cultivated land.' Then Ibrahim said, 'tell him (Ismail), "a sheikh came after you have left and said, 'I found the threshold of your house to be good, so you should keep it."' When Ismail came back to his house he asked his wife, 'has anyone came after I left?' She said, 'yes, a sheikh came,' and then she described him. Ismail asked, 'did he tell you anything?' She said, 'yes, he said, "I found the threshold of your house to be good, so keep it."'"

---

30. The al-Mubtada' book, meaning 'The Book of Beginning,' likely refers to the first book of the Torah, Genesis.

Ibrahim Builds the Ka'ba and Sets the Black Stone

51 - Abu al-Walid narrated to us, saying, my grandfather narrated to me, saying, Muslim ibn Khalid al-Zanji narrated to us, on the authority of Ibn Jurayj, on the authority of Kathir ibn Kathir, on the authority of Sa'id ibn Jubayr, who said, Ibn Abbas narrated to us, saying:

"Ibrahim stayed away for as much time as Allah willed; then he visited for the third time and found Ismail sitting under the big tree that is near the well, sharpening [or mending] some spears. Ibrahim greeted Ismail and sat next to him. Ibrahim said, 'oh Ismail, Allah has ordered me to do something.' Ismail said, 'obey Allah and do what he ordered you to do.' Ibrahim said, 'Allah has ordered me to build a house for him.' Ismail asked, 'where?'"

Ibn Abbas said: "he (Ibrahim) pointed to a hill covered with fine gravel; when the floods come, [the water] runs around the sides [of the hill] and does not cover it."

Ibn Abbas said: "they both started digging the foundations and said, 'our Lord, accept this from us; You are the Hearer of prayers. Oh Lord, accept this from us; You are the All Hearer the All Knower.' Ismail was the one who carried the stones on his shoulders, and sheikh Ibrahim built. Then when the building became higher and Ibrahim could no longer lift the stones, Ismail brought a stone, al-Maqam.[31] Ibrahim stood on it and continued building all sides of the House until he finished it."

Ibn Abbas said: "for that reason, the stone was called al-Maqam, because Ibrahim was standing on it."

52 - Mahdi ibn Abi al-Mahdi narrated to me, saying, Abdullah ibn Ma'adh al-San'ani narrated to us, on the authority of Ma'mar, on the authority of Ayyub al-Sakhtiyani, and Kathir ibn Kathir, one adding to the other, on the authority of Sa'id ibn Jubayr, in a long hadith narrated about Ibn Abbas, who said:

"Ibrahim came while Ismail was mending his spears under the Doha (large tree) near Zamzam. When Ismail saw his father, he quickly stood up and went to greet him, and they did what fathers do to their children, and what children do to their fathers."

Mua'mir said: "I have heard a man who said, 'they wept until the birds answered them.'"

Sa'id said: "he (Ibrahim) said, 'oh Ismail, Allah the Almighty has ordered me to do something.' Ismail said, 'obey Allah in His orders.' Ibrahim said, 'will you help me?' Ismail said, 'I will.' Ibrahim said, 'Allah the Almighty has ordered me to build him a house here.' After that Ibrahim raised the foundations of the House."

53 - My grandfather narrated to me, saying, Sa'id ibn Salim narrated to us, who said, Ibn Jurayj informed me, who said, Mujahid said:

---

31. The Maqam Ibrahim, or Station of Ibrahim, is believed to feature the imprint of Ibrahim's feet and is venerated to this day.

"Ibrahim came along with al-Sakina, al-Sard, and al-Malak from al-Sham.[32] Al-Sakina said, 'oh Ibrahim, stay close to the House, so that there will be no king nor a Bedouin circumambulating the House except [if] you see a Sakina on them.'"[33]

The narrator continued, and Ibn Jarih said: 'al-Sakina came with him; it had a head like a cat's head and two wings."

54 - My grandfather narrated to me, on the authority of Sa'id ibn Salim, on the authority of Uthman ibn Saj, on the authority of Ibn Jurayj, who said, Ali ibn Abi Talib said:

"Ibrahim came along with al-Malak, al-Sakina, and al-Sard, which guided him until he reached the place of the Forbidden House [Bayt Haram]. Like a spider spins its web, he started digging until he uncovered a prominent rock, like a pregnant camel. The rock could only be moved by 30 men."

Ali continued: "then [Allah] said to Ibrahim, 'get up and build me a house.' Ibrahim asked, 'oh Lord, where?' He said, 'we will show you.'"

Ali continued: "Allah the Almighty sent a cloud with a head, talking to Ibrahim. [It] said, 'oh Ibrahim, Allah has ordered you to draw a line the size of this cloud.' So, Ibrahim kept looking at (the cloud) and drew its measurements. Then the head asked, 'have you finished?' Ibrahim said, 'yes.' After that, the cloud rose to the sky. Then a firm foundation was unveiled from the earth, and Ibrahim built on top of it."

55 - He said, my grandfather narrated to me, on the authority of Sa'id ibn Salim, on the authority of Uthman ibn Saj, who said, Muḥammad ibn Abban informed me, on the authority of Ibn Ishaq al-Sabi'i, on the authority of Harithah ibn Mudarrib, on the authority of Ali ibn Abi Talib, in a hadith he narrated about Zamzam, saying:

"Then al-Sakina came down like a cloud or fog; the middle of it was shaped like a speaking head. It said, 'oh Ibrahim, copy my size on the earth—no more, no less.' So, Ibrahim drew the lines, and that is Becca, and what is around it is Mecca."[34]

56 - My grandfather narrated to me, on the authority of Sa'id ibn Salim, on the authority of Uthman ibn Saj, on the authority of Wahb ibn Munabbih, who informed him, saying:

"When Allah the Almighty had sent His Khalil Ibrahim to build him a house, [Ibrahim] searched for the first foundation that was laid by Adam's sons at the place of the tent that Allah sent down to Adam from Paradise to console him. It was positioned in Mecca at the place of the Forbidden House. Ibrahim kept digging until he reached the foundation that Adam's sons laid at the place of the tent, then Allah shaded the place of the House with a cloud that extended to the edges of the House. The cloud remained there, providing shade for Ibrahim and guiding

---

32. "Al-Sham" could refer to 'north' or 'Damascus.' Gibson prefers 'north.'
33. Passage 57 reads that al-Sakina (السكينة) was a whirlwind. The Arabic term al-Sard refers to a high drifting cloud (cirrus). The term al-Malak is translated as angel, as in guardian angel.
34. Azraqi mentions Becca and Mecca as two different places. Becca, which means weeping, may refer to the valley where Hajar wept before she located Zamzam. Mecca, on the other hand, seems to have referred to a larger sacred area, possibly the entire area marked by the great rocks.

him to the place of the foundations, until he raised the height of the foundations. Then it (the cloud) was removed. That is what Allah the Almighty said (in the Qur'an), "*We assigned for Ibrahim the place of the House*," referring to the cloud the was resting on top of the House's location to show Ibrahim the place of the foundations (Qur'an 22:26). And Alhamdulillah,[35] it is still frequented since the day Allah raised it."

57 - Mahdi ibn Abi al-Mahdi narrated to me, saying, Abdul Rahman ibn Abdullah, the freedman of Banu Hashim, narrated to us, saying, Hammad informed us, on the authority of Simak ibn Harb, on the authority of Khalid ibn Ar'arah, on the authority of Ali ibn Abi Talib, regarding the saying of the Almighty, "*truly the first House established for mankind was that at Bakkah, full of blessing and a guidance for the worlds*" (Qur'an 3:96). He said:

"It is not the first house; Adam dwelled in houses before Ibrahim did, and Ibrahim dwelled in houses as well, but it is the first house established for mankind with evident signs: the Maqam of Ibrahim. Whoever enters it will attain security. These are the verses."

Then he said: "Ibrahim was ordered to build the house. His arms became tired, and he did not know how to build it. Therefore, Allah the Almighty sent him al-Sakina, which was a strong whirlwind, and it spun around like an enclosure or fence. So, Ibrahim started building around it. Every day he built one row of blocks, and Mecca was very hot at that time.

"When he reached to the place of the stone (the Corner) he said to Ismail, 'go and find me a rock to place here, in order to guide people.' Ismail roamed the mountains, and then Jibril came to Ismail with the Black Stone and Ismail asked, 'where did you get this stone from?' He said, 'from the one who does not rely on my building or your building [skills].'

"It (the House) then collapsed, and was rebuilt by the Amalekites [A'maliqa], and collapsed again, and was rebuilt by a tribe from the Jurhum, and collapsed again, and was rebuilt by the Quraysh. When they (the Quraysh) wanted to place the Stone back in its position, they disagreed (on who would place it), so they said, 'the first man who enters from this door will place it.' The prophet Muhammad was the first to enter. He asked them to bring him a piece of cloth; he laid it down and placed the Stone on it, then he said, 'a man from each tribe will come and hold a corner of the cloth,' and they all held the cloth together. Then the prophet himself placed it back in its position."

58 - My grandfather narrated to me, saying, Sufyan ibn Uyaynah narrated to me, on the authority of Bishr ibn Asim, on the authority of Sa'id ibn al-Musayyib, who said, Ali ibn Abi Talib informed me, saying:

"Ibrahim came from Armenia, with al-Sakina guiding him until he settled down in the House, just like spiders settle in their webs, and they (Ibrahim and Ismail) started building on top of the stones. The one stone could take up to 30 men to move."

---

35. "All praise and gratitude be to Allah."

59 - Mahdi ibn Abi al-Mahdi narrated to me, saying, Abdullah ibn Ma'adh al-San'ani narrated to us, on the authority of Ma'mar, on the authority of Qatta'dah, regarding the verse, *"[remember] when Ibrahim and Ishmael were raising the foundations of the House, 'our Lord, accept [it] from us. Truly Thou art the Hearing, the Knowing'"* (Qur'an 2:127). He said:

"[The stones] were the foundations of the House before that."

Al-Khuza'i said: "Abu Ubaydellah has narrated a similar account, on the authority of Sufyan ibn Uyana."

60 - Mahdi ibn Abi al-Mahdi narrated to us, saying, Abdul Rahman ibn Abdullah, the freedman of Banu Hashim, narrated to us, saying, Abu Awanah narrated to us, on the authority of Ibn Abi Bishr, on the authority of Sa'id ibn Jubayr, on the authority of Ibn Abbas, who said:

"By Allah, they did not build it with mud nor with plaster, and they did not have enough money or helpers to put a roof on it, but they established it as a sign and did tawaf around it."

61 - My grandfather narrated to me, saying, Sufyan ibn Uyaynah narrated to us, on the authority of Mujalid, on the authority of al-Sha'bi, who said:

"When Ibrahim was ordered to build the House, and as he reached to the place of the Stone (the Corner), he said to Ismail, 'bring me a stone to put as a starting point for people.' He brought him a stone, but Ibrahim could not break it. Then he (Ibrahim) came with the current Stone and said, 'this was given to me by the One who did not make me rely on your stone.'"

62 - My grandfather narrated to me, saying, Dawud ibn Abdul Rahman narrated to us, on the authority of Ibn Jurayj, on the authority of Bishr ibn Asim, who said:

"Ibrahim came from Armenia, with al-Sakina, al-Malak, and al-Sard to guide him to the place of the House where he could settle down, just like a spider settles in its house. He lifted a stone, which was then carried by 30 people, and al-Sakina said, 'build around me, so there will be no fugitive Bedouin nor an arrogant man circumambulating the House except that you see tranquility [or Sakina] on them.'"

63 - Mahdi ibn Abi al-Mahdi narrated to me, saying, Bishr ibn al-Sari al-Basri narrated to us, on the authority of Hammad ibn Zayd, on the authority of Ayyub, on the authority of Abu Qilabah, who said:

"Allah the Almighty said, 'oh Adam, I sent My House down with you. Tawaf will be done around it just like the tawaf that is done around My Throne, and prayers will be held at it just like the prayers at My Throne.' The conditions remained like this until the time of the flood when the House was raised up. Then its place was shown to Ibrahim who built it from the stones of five mountains: Hara,[36] Thabir,[37] Lubnan,[38] At-toor,[39] and the red mountain."

---

36. Possibly a mythical Iranian mountain, or a reference to all the mountains of Iran.
37. Likely Jebal Thawer, a mountain in Mecca where the cave of Muḥammad was located.
38. The mountains of Lebanon.
39. Meaning 'the mountain.' This is the name of Surah 52, wherein Allah swears by 'the mount,' possibly Mount Sinai or Horeb where the Tawrat (Torah) was revealed to Musa (Moses).

64 - Mahdi ibn Abi al-Mahdi narrated to me, saying, Umar ibn Sahl narrated to us, on the authority of Yazid ibn Zuray', on the authority of Sa'id, on the authority of Qatta'dah, regarding the saying of the Almighty, *"[remember] when Ibrahim and Ishmael were raising the foundations of the House"* (Qur'an 2:127). He said:

"It was mentioned to us that he (Ibrahim) built it from five mountains: from Toor Sinaa,[40] Toor Zita,[41] Lubnan,[42] al-Judi,[43] and Hara,[44] and it was mentioned to us that its foundations are from Hira.[45]"

65 - Mahdi ibn Abi al-Mahdi narrated to me, saying, Marwan ibn Mu'awiyah al-Fazari narrated to us, saying, al-Ala narrated to us, on the authority of Umar ibn Murrah, on the authority of Yusuf ibn Mahak, who said, Abdullah ibn Amr said:

"Jibril was the one who brought the Stone down to Ibrahim from Paradise and placed it where you have seen it. You will remain prosperous as long as you still have it amongst you, so hold fast to it as much as you can, as he (Jibril) is about to come and return it to where it came from."

66 - My grandfather narrated to me, on the authority of Sa'id ibn Salim, on the authority of Uthman ibn Saj, who said, Muḥammad ibn Ishaq informed me, saying:

"when Ibrahim Khalil Allah was ordered to build the Forbidden House he came from Armenia riding al-Buraq, and al-Sakina was with him. It was a strong breeze and had a talking face. There was also an angel with him showing him the [way to] place of the House, until he reached Mecca. At that time, Ismail was there (at Mecca) and he was 20 years old. His mother died before that, and she was buried at the place of the stone [al-hijr].[46] Ibrahim said, 'oh Ismail, Allah has ordered me to build him a house.' Ismail said, 'where it will be?'

The narrator continued: "the angel then indicated the direction of the House. They both started digging the foundations, with no one else with them, until Ibrahim reached the first foundation that Adam laid. He found great stones; one of them could only be moved by 30 men. Ibrahim built upon the first foundation of Adam, then al-Sakina circled around the first foundation like a snake and said, 'oh Ibrahim, build on me,' and so he did. [Because of] that, anyone who does tawaf around the House, either a fleeting Bedouin or an oppressor, you will see tranquility upon him.

---

40. Toor Sinaa could refer to Mount Horeb (28.555948° 33.976048°) or Jebal al-Lawz (28.654107° 35.305831°).
41. Or the Mount of Olives: 31.777908° 35.245685°.
42. The mountains of Lebanon.
43. Al-Judi is a mountain in Turkey, regarded as the resting place of the ark: 37.370292° 42.496901°.
44. Possibly a mythical Iranian mountain, or a reference to all the mountains of Iran.
45. This word is not the same as the Hira in passage 10. In this case, Hira may refer to the cave where Muḥammad received his revelation. The mountain containing the cave has several names, including Jebal Thawer mentioned above; in Mecca today it is known as Jebal Nour (mountain of light).
46. This stone is known today at the 'Stone of Ismail.'

"Then Ibrahim built the House, and he made it nine cubits tall toward the sky and thirty-two cubits wide on earth from the Black Corner to the Shami Corner which faces the Hijr. And he made its width between the Shami Corner and the Western Corner, where the Hijr is located, twenty-two cubits. The back side from the Western Corner to the Yemeni Corner was thirty-one cubits, and the width of the Yemeni side, which is between the Black Stone and the Yemeni Corner was twenty cubits. Therefore, it was called Ka'ba, as it takes the shape of a Kaab [or cube, كعب].

If we calculate a cubit as 0.53 meters, then Azraqi's dimensions for the Ka'ba are 17 meters, 11.6 meters, 16.4 meters, and 10.6 meters. These measurements are approximate since the size of a cubit varied over time.

The Petra altar, with the stairs included as part of the structure, matches Azraqi's description of the Ka'ba. Note that the ruined altar in Petra is irregularly shaped, just as Azraqi describes.

The Mecca Ka'ba differs from Azraqi's measurements in length, while the width is quite similar. Note the Mecca Ka'ba is the same size and shape as the altar in Petra, but without the stairs. The Petra altar is so ruined and the corners so damaged that exact measurements are not possible.

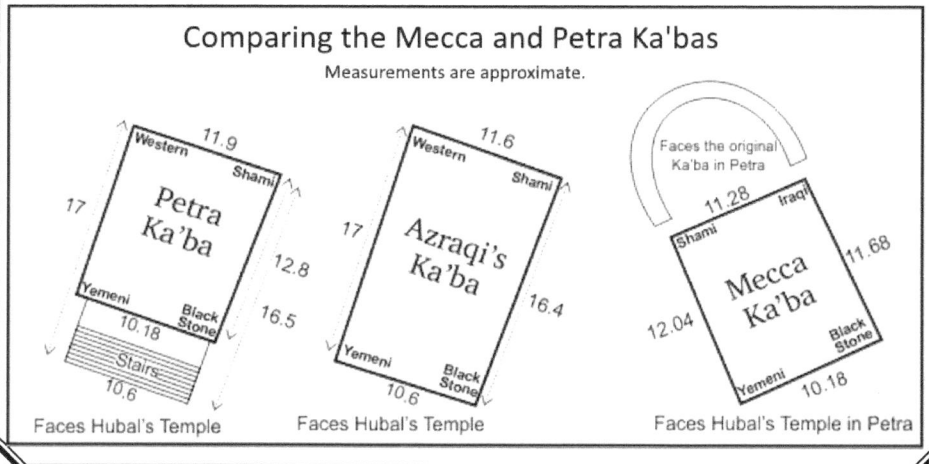

The narrator continued: "[it] was similar to the construction of Adam's foundation, and he (Ibrahim) made the Ka'ba's entrance at ground-level without a door. It remained like that until the time of Tubba' Asa'd al-Humairi, who put a door on the Ka'ba with a Persian latch, and draped it with kiswah[47] and slaughtered an animal near it."

---

47. The covering cloth of the Ka'ba, كسوة.

The narrator continued: "Ibrahim shaded the hijr next to the House with arak trees, which were frequently broken into by goats. It was a pasture for Ismail's sheep."

The narrator continued: "Ibrahim dug a well[48] inside the House. It was on the right when entering the Ka'ba, to serve as a storing place for the House where the gifts that are given to the Ka'ba are thrown. This well is the one which was used by Amr ibn Luhi to erect Hubal, the idol that was worshipped by the Quraysh, who also used it for foretelling and receiving omens. This idol was brought from Heet,[49] in the Arabian Peninsula."

The narrator said: "Ibrahim was building the House, and Ismail was carrying the rocks on his shoulders to him. When the building grew higher, Ismail brought the Maqam to him, so he (Ibrahim) could stand on it and build. Then Ismail moved it for him around the House until they reached the place of the Black Corner where Ibrahim said to Ismail, 'oh Ismail, I need a stone here to guide people and serve as a starting point for tawaf.' Ismail went looking for a stone. When he came back, he found the Black Stone brought by Jibril. Allah the Almighty entrusted the Corner to Aba Kobais[50] during the flood at the time of Noah. He (Allah) said, 'if you see My Khalil building My House, get [the Black Stone] out for him.'"

The narrator said: "then Ismail came, and he said, 'oh father, from where did you get this?' Ibrahim said, 'it has been brought to me by the one who did not make me rely on your stone. It has been brought by Jibril.' Jibril placed the Stone in its position, and Ibrahim completed the building around it, and [the Stone] was at that time sparkling pure white, so intense that it shone in all directions: east, west, Yemen, and Sham."[51]

The narrator continued: "it is now black because it has been burned repeatedly, in the pre-Islamic time and after Islam. The fire that happened in the pre-Islamic time was caused by a woman at the time of the Quraysh. She burned incense (to perfume the Ka'ba), and a spark flew off from her live coal into the Ka'ba's curtains, and the Ka'ba burned. The Black Corner was also burned and turned black because of that, and the whole structure of the Ka'ba became very weak. That incident led the Quraysh to tear down the Ka'ba and rebuild it. Regarding the fire that happened after Islam, it was during the days of Ibn al-Zubayr, when he was besieged by al-Hussein ibn Numair al-Kindi. The Ka'ba was burned, and the Corner was burned as well, and it cracked into three parts. Ibn al-Zubayr strengthened it with a silver frame. Therefore, the Stone turned to black."

The narrator continued: "if the Corner was not touched by the impurity and filth of the pre-Islamic time, it would have been a cure to anyone who touches it, who sufferers a bodily defect."

---

48. The word for 'well,' *beer*, can also mean cistern.
49. Heet or Hit Iraq, located: 33.643596° 42.823963°.
50. A mountain.
51. "Yemen and Sham" mean south and north, respectively.

67 - Sa'id ibn Salim said that Ibn Jurayj said:

"Ibn al-Zubayr rebuilt the Ka'ba and made it the same size (measured in cubits) as was done by Ibrahim."

He continued: "it is cubical like a cube, and for that reason it was called [the] Ka'ba."

He added: "Ibrahim did not put a roof on the Ka'ba, and he did not build it with mud [or mud bricks]. Instead, he used great stones that were compressed together."

> The Second Islamic Civil War, 680-692 CE or 61-73 AH, was a conflict between the Umayyad caliphate and challengers to the caliphate, such as Abd Allah ibn al-Zubayr ibn al-Awaam. Ibn al-Zubayr controlled Mecca when he rebelled against the Umayyads. His rebellion led to two sieges of Mecca; the second siege, led by general al-Hajjaj ibn Yusuf, resulted in Ibn al-Zubayr's death and the destruction of the Ka'ba.
>
> During the first siege the Ka'ba was damaged and needed to be rebuilt. Ibn al-Zubayr's efforts to repair the Ka'ba are detailed above and in entry 19.
>
> All extant mosque qiblas from the time of the Second Civil War are directed toward Petra. This archaeological evidence suggests that Ibn al-Zubayr's 'Mecca' and the seat of his rebellion was the city of Petra. This perspective is further supported by evidence of manjaniq (small trebuchet) stones in the ruins of Petra, exactly as described by Islamic historians.
>
> Dan Gibson believes that between the two Umayyad sieges of the Holy City, Ibn al-Zubayr moved the Black Stone from the Ka'ba down into the Hijaz to protect it from further sieges and prevent its seizure by the Umayyads. It was this effort which eventually led to the entire relocation of the Holy City to a remote place in the Hijaz.[52]

---

68 - My grandfather narrated to me, saying, Sufyan ibn Uyaynah narrated to us, on the authority of Ibn Abi Najih, on the authority of Mujahid, who said:

"Al-Sakina had a head that looked like a cat's head, and two wings."

69 - Mahdi ibn Abi al-Mahdi narrated to me, saying, Bishr ibn al-Sari narrated to us, saying, Qais ibn al-Rabi' narrated to us, on the authority of Salamah ibn Kuhayl, on the authority of Abu al-Ahwas, on the authority of Ali ibn Hafafah, who said:

"Al-Sakina had a head that looked like a man's head. It turned into a strong breeze after that."

---

52. Dan Gibson, *Let the Stones Speak: Archaeology Challenges Islam* (Saskatoon: CanBooks, 2023), 125ff.

70 - Mahdi ibn Abi al-Mahdi narrated to us, saying, al-Fazari narrated to us, on the authority of Juwaybir, on the authority of al-Dahhak, who said:

"Al-Sakina is mercy."

Ibrahim Calls the World to Hajj and the Prophets Respond

71 - Abu al-Walid narrated to us, saying, my grandfather narrated to me, on the authority of Sa'id ibn Salim, on the authority of Uthman ibn Saj, who said, Muḥammad ibn Ishaq informed me, saying: "When Ibrahim had finished building the Forbidden House, Jibril came to him and said, 'circumambulate around the House seven times.' Ibrahim did so with Ismail; they touched every corner in each tawaf, and when they finished the seven rounds, they both prayed two Raka'at behind the Maqam."

The narrator continued: "then Jibril showed Ibrahim all the rituals: Safa and Marwa, Mina, Muzdalifah, and 'Arafat."[53]

The narrator added: "then when he entered Mina and came down the hill,[54] Iblis[55] appeared to him at J'amrat[56] al-A'qaba.[57] Jibril said to Ibrahim, 'throw stones at him,' so Ibrahim threw seven pebbles at Iblis who disappeared after that. Iblis reappeared to Ibrahim at the middle J'amrah, and Jibril said, 'throw stones at him,' so Ibrahim again threw seven pebbles at Iblis until he disappeared. Iblis reappeared again at the lower J'amrah, and Jibril said, 'throw stones at him,' and Ibrahim threw seven pebbles until Iblis disappeared. Ibrahim continued his pilgrimage, with Jibril stopping him at each destination and teaching him the rituals, until Ibrahim arrived at 'Arafat. When he reached there, Jibril asked, 'have you learned your rituals?' Ibrahim replied, 'yes.'"

The narrator added: "it was called 'Arafat because of Jibril's saying, 'have you learned your rituals?'"[58]

The narrator said: "after that, Ibrahim was commanded to proclaim the pilgrimage to humanity. Ibrahim said, 'oh Lord, will my voice reach them?' Allah the Almighty responded, 'your duty is to proclaim and My duty is to convey.'"

The narrator continued: "Ibrahim then stood over the Maqam, which ascended until it became the tallest and greatest of mountains. The whole earth was ordered to gather for him: the hills, the mountains, the land, the seas, mankind, and the jinn, until they were all able to hear him."

---

53. "Safa and Marwa" refers to the ritual of walking or running between the two mountains. Mina involves sleeping in the valley of Mina and throwing stones at the pillars. 'Arafat refers to standing on the mountain top, contemplating God. Muzdalifah is the ritual of coming down from the mountain in the dark. The intention of this passage is to associate these rituals with Ibrahim, and not a later development of the pagans of Mecca.
54. Or al-A'qaba, العقبة.
55. The devil; the parallel of Satan in Christianity.
56. J'amrat literally means pebbles but has come to represent the stone pillars used to ritually stone the devil during the Hajj.
57. J'amrat al-A'qaba is also the name of the ritual of throwing stones.
58. A'raft, عرفت, is an Arabic word that means 'have you learned?'

He continued: "then Ibrahim put his two fingers in his ears, and faced Yemen, and Sham, and east, and west. He started with the Yemen side and said, 'oh people, you have been ordered to go on pilgrimage to the Ancient House, so respond to the call of your Lord.' Everything between east and west, and between earth and heaven, to the ends of earth answered his call (saying the Talbiyah), '*I am at Your service, oh Allah, I am at Your service.*'"[59]

The narrator added: "the stone [or Maqam] was as it is today, but Allah the Almighty wanted to make the stone a sign, so the imprint of Ibrahim's feet remained on the stone until this day."

He added: "do you not hear people say '*I am at Your service, oh Allah, I am at Your service*'? Therefore, anyone who performs pilgrimage up to this day is among those who have answered Ibrahim, and their pilgrimage is equal to their response, so those who have done pilgrimage twice, they have answered the call of Ibrahim twice, and if they did it three times then they have answered him three times, and so on."

The narrator said: "and the imprint of Ibrahim's feet on the Maqam is a sign, as Allah the Almighty said, '*therein are clear signs: the station of Ibrahim, and whosoever enters it shall be secure*' (Qur'an 3:97).

Ibn Ishaq said: "I have heard that Adam touched all the corners before Ibrahim, and that Sara and Ishaq had come from al-Sham to perform pilgrimage."

He added: "and Ibrahim came every year to perform Hajj, riding al-Buraq. After that the prophets and the nations have also performed Hajj."

72 - My grandfather narrated to me, saying, Ibn Uyaynah narrated to us, on the authority of Ibn Abi Najih, on the authority of Mujahid, who said:
"Ibrahim and Ismail came on foot to perform Hajj."

Abu Muḥammad Ubaydullah al-Makhzumi said: "Ibn Uyana has narrated a similar account."

73 - Al-Azraqi narrated to us, saying, my grandfather narrated to me, saying, Yahya ibn Salim narrated to us, on the authority of Ibn Khuthaym, who said, I heard Abdul Rahman ibn Sabit say:
"Between the Corner and the Maqam and Zamzam are the graves of 99 prophets who came to perform Hajj, and they were buried there."

74 - Mahdi ibn Abi al-Mahdi narrated to me, saying, Abdul Rahman ibn Abdullah, the freedman of Banu Hashim, narrated to us, on the authority of Hammad Salamah, on the authority of Atta' ibn al-Sa'ib, on the authority of Muḥammad ibn Sabit, on the authority of the prophet, who said:
"When Allah destroys a nation (as a punishment) their prophet comes to Mecca to worship Allah with the believers from his nation, until he dies there. Noah, Hud,

---

59. The Talbiyah is a ritual prayer, part of the pilgrimages.

Saleh, and Shoaib[60] have all died there, and their graves are between Zamzam and the Hijr."[61]

75 - My grandfather narrated to me, saying, Sa'id ibn Salim narrated to us, on the authority of Uthman ibn Saj, on the authority of Khasif, on the authority of Mujahid, who said:
"Prophet Musa[62] came to Hajj riding a red camel, passing by al-Rouhaa.[63] He had two cotton cloaks, one of them wrapped around the lower part of his body and he wore the other. Musa did tawaf around the House and between Safa and Marwa. When he was still between Safa and Marwa, he heard a voice coming from heaven saying: 'here I Am, My slave. I Am with you.' Musa fell into prostration out of gratitude."

76 - My grandfather narrated to me, saying, Sa'id ibn Salim narrated to us, on the authority of Uthman ibn Saj, on the authority of Khasif, on the authority of Mujahid, who said:
"75 prophets had performed Hajj; all of them did tawaf around the House and prayed at Mina Mosque.[64] If you can, do not miss a prayer at Mina Mosque."

77 - My grandfather narrated to me, saying, Marwan ibn Mu'awiyah narrated to us, on the authority of al-Ash'ath ibn Sawar, on the authority of Ikrimah, on the authority of Ibn Abbas, who said:
"70 prophets prayed at al-Kheef mosque; all of them used (palm) fiber as a bridle."

Marwan ibn Mu'awiyah explained: "He (Ibn Abbas) meant the animals they were riding."

78 - My grandfather narrated to me, saying, Sa'id ibn Salim narrated to us, on the authority of Uthman ibn Saj, who said, Khasif ibn Abdul Rahman informed us, on the authority of Mujahid, who told him, saying:
"When Ibrahim said, 'oh our Lord, show us our rites,' he was ordered to raise the foundations of the House, then he was shown al-Safa and al-Marwa, and was told this is from Allah's rituals."

The narrator continued: "then Jibril went out with him, and when they passed by J'amrat al-A'qaba they found Iblis there. Jibril said, 'say Takbir[65] and throw stones at him.' Iblis then moved to the middle J'amrah, and Jibril said, 'say Takbir and throw stones at him.' Iblis moved to the lower J'amrah and Jibril said, 'say Takbir and throw stones at him.' After that they went to the Sacred Ritual, and then to

---

60. A Midianite prophet, associated with the prophet Jethro in the Torah. Information on his shrine can be found here: https://www.islamiclandmarks.com/jordan/maqam-of-prophet-shoayb-as
61. In contradiction to this passage, the traditional burial places of Hud, Saleh, and Shoaib are not in Mecca in the Hijaz.
62. The parallel of Moses in Christianity, Moshe in Judaism.
63. Al-Rouhaa, الروحاء, is an ancient name for a narrow sacred path through the mountains.
64. Masjid Mina is also known as Masjid al-Khayf (مسجد الخيف). In Mecca in Saudi Arabia, Masjid Mina is located at the foot of a mountain in the south of Mina, close to the smallest Jamarat. It is claimed that at this spot Muhammad and other prophets before him performed salah; thus, it is also known as the 'Mosque of the prophets'. In essence, it was a small place of prayer next to Mina.
65. The Arabic name of the declaration, "Allahu Akhbar."

'Arafat. Jibril asked, 'have you learned what you have seen?' and repeated that three times. Ibrahim responded, 'yes.' Jibril said, 'proclaim Hajj to mankind.' Ibrahim asked, 'what should I say?' Jibril said, 'you say, "oh people, answer your Lord's call," three times.'"

The narrator continued: "they (the people) said, *'at Your service, oh Allah, at Your service.'* Anyone who answered Ibrahim's call is a pilgrim."

Khasif said: "when Mujahid told me this he said, 'the people of Kadr do not believe in this hadith.'"

79 - My grandfather narrated to me, saying, Uthman said, Musa ibn Ubaydah informed me, saying: "When Ibrahim was ordered to announce pilgrimage to humanity, he moved around the earth and called people at every side saying, 'oh people, answer your Lord's call and perform Hajj.'"

The narrator said: "people answered his call from every east and every west. The mountains were bowed down until his voice lowered (as he traveled farther away)."

80 - Uthman said, Ibn Jurayj informed me, saying, Ibn Abbas said:
"*They shall come to thee on foot and upon all [manner of] lean beast, coming from all deep and distant mountain highways*" (Qur'an 22:27).

Another one said: "they will come on foot, walking on their feet. *'And upon all lean beast'* means any camel that enters the Sanctuary is a transport. *'They will come from all deep and distant mountain highways'* means faraway places."

Atta' said: "*'and show us our rites'* means make the rites distinguished to us and teach them to us (Qur'an 2:128)."

Mujahid said: "*'And show us our rites'* means our sacrifice or oblation."

81 - He said, Uthman ibn Saj informed me, saying, Muḥammad ibn Ishaq informed me, saying: "I have been told by some scholars that Abdullah ibn al-Zubayr asked Ubayd ibn Umair al-Laythi, 'how did you know that Ibrahim called for Hajj?' He replied, 'I have heard that when Ibrahim and Ismail raised the foundations and fulfilled Allah's command on that matter, it was the time for Hajj. Ibrahim faced the direction of Yemen and called people to follow Allah the Almighty and to perform Hajj in the House. His call was answered by people saying, *"at Your service, O Allah, at Your service."* Then he faced the eastern direction and called [people] to follow Allah and perform Hajj. His call was answered with, *"at Your service, at Your service."* He did the same facing the west, then facing the direction of Sham. After that, he performed Hajj with Ismail and the believers from Jurhum, who were the inhabitants of the Sanctuary at that time with Ismail and [Ismail's] relatives by marriage. Ibrahim then led them in praying Dhuhur [noon], Asr [afternoon], Maghrib [sunset], and Ishaa [night] in Mina. They all spent the night there until morning when Ibrahim led them in praying Fajr [dawn]. Afterward, they went to Namira[66]

---
66. Namira means a place of water.

and stayed there. When the sun declined, he combined the prayers of Dhuhur and Asr in the Mosque of Ibrahim on 'Arafat.[67] Later he led them to the place of halting [Mawqif] at 'Arafat and stayed there. This place is the halting place of the Imam[68] in 'Arafat where he showed [the rituals] and taught [Ibrahim]. After the sunset, they all moved to Muzdalifah[69] and he led the prayers of Maghrib and Ishaa combined. They spent the night there until the time of Fajr when he led them in Fajr prayer. Then they stood on Quzah in Muzdalifah,[70] which is the halting place of the Imam, until the daylight appeared, before sunrise, when he and all those with him were shown how to throw pebbles [Jimar]. When they had finished all the Hajj rituals, Ibrahim went back to al-Sham where he died, peace be upon him and upon all prophets of Allah."

82 - Uthman said, Ibn Ishaq informed me, saying:
"Allah the Almighty ordered Ibrahim to perform Hajj and to announce it (and show it) to people. The Almighty showed Ibrahim the rituals of the House and laid down the religious obligations to him. At that time, when Ibrahim was given this command, he was at Bayt al-Maqdis from Ayliya."[71]

83 - Uthman said, Zuhayr ibn Muḥammad informed me, saying:
"When Ibrahim finished building the Forbidden House he said, 'oh Lord, I did as You commanded. Show us our rituals.' Allah the Almighty sent Jibril who did Hajj with Ibrahim. When the day of sacrifice [Nahr, النحر] came, Iblis was shown to Ibrahim. Then Jibril said, 'throw at him.' So, he threw seven pebbles at Iblis. Then he (did the same) the next day, and the third day, until he filled up what is between the two mountains. Afterward, he stood on Thabir[72] and said, 'oh slaves of Allah, answer the call of your Lord.' His call was heard from beyond the seas, and those who have a speck of faith in their hearts said, *'at your service, oh Allah, at your service.'*"

He continued: "the presence of seven Muslims or more will not discontinue on the surface of this earth. Had it not been for this, the earth and everything on it would have been destroyed."

84 - Uthman said, Zuhayr ibn Muḥammad informed me:
"The first to answer Ibrahim's call to perform Hajj were the people of Yemen."[73]

---

67. An ancient place of prayer on 'Arafat.
68. Probably referring to Jibril.
69. A slippery slope descending from mount 'Arafat.
70. A stopping place along the slippery slope of Muzdalifah.
71. Ayliya means ascension, usually referring to the approach to Jerusalem.
72. A mountain near Mecca.
73. At various times, Yemen included all southern Arabia, up to Medina. It is impossible to know what "Yemen" included in this instance.

85 - My grandfather informed me, on the authority of Sa'id ibn Salim, on the authority of Uthman ibn Saj, who said, Uthman ibn al-Aswad informed me, on the authority of Atta' ibn Abi Rabah:
"Musa ibn Omran did tawaf between al-Safa and al-Marwa, and he was wearing a cotton cloak and saying, '*at your service, oh Allah, at your service.*' Allah the Almighty answered him, 'here I am, Musa; I Am with you.'"

86 - My grandfather informed me, on the authority of Sa'id ibn Salim, on the authority of Uthman ibn Saj, who said, Ghalib ibn Ubayd Allah narrated to me, saying, I heard Mujahid mention on the authority of Ibn Abbas, who said:
"60 prophets have passed by Sifah al-Rouhaa.[74] Their camels were bridled with palm fiber."

87 - Uthman said, Ghalib ibn Ubayd Allah informed me, saying, I heard Mujahid mention on the authority of Ibn Abbas, who said:
"Prophet Musa came while reciting the Talbiyah and the mountains of al-Sham answered [or echoed] him. He was riding a red camel and wearing two cotton cloaks."

88 - Uthman said, Ibn Ishaq informed me, saying, someone I do not accuse of lying told me, on the authority of Urwah ibn al-Zubayr, who said:
"I have heard that the House was sent to Adam [that he may] circumambulate around it and worship Allah, and that Noah visited it and did Hajj at it before the flood. When the earth drowned and the people of Noah perished the House was equally affected by what happened to the earth, and its place was a red hill at that time. Allah the Almighty sent the prophet Hud to the people of A'ad; he was very busy with his people until he died without performing Hajj. Then Allah the Almighty sent prophet Saleh to the people of Thamud and he became very busy with the issues of his people and died before visiting the House and performing Hajj. Afterwards, the place of the House was revealed to prophet Ibrahim, who performed Hajj at it and was taught its rituals. He announced the Hajj to mankind and called for people to visit [the House]. All prophets who Allah sent after Ibrahim have performed Hajj."

89 - Uthman said, Ibn Ishaq informed me, saying, someone I do not accuse of lying told me on the authority of Sa'id ibn al-Musayyib, on the authority of a man who was a scholar, who used to say:
"As if I am looking at Musa ibn Omran coming down the Hirsha,[75] wearing a cotton cloak and reciting Talbiyah for his Hajj."

90 - Uthman said, Muḥammad ibn Ishaq informed me, saying, someone I do not accuse of lying told me, on the authority of Allah's [servant] Ibn Abbas, who used to say:

---

74. Here the word 'stone' or 'flagstone' is added to describe the ancient sacred path to Mecca through the mountains.
75. The name of a sacred mountain road.

"70 prophets have passed through the route of Rouhaa to perform Hajj. They were wearing wool clothes and their camels were bridled with palm fiber ropes. And 70 prophets have prayed at al-Kheef mosque."

91 - My grandfather narrated to me, saying, Uthman ibn Saj said, Muḥammad ibn Ishaq informed me, and Talhah said, Ubayd Allah ibn Kurayz al-Khuza'i narrated to me:
"When Musa performed Hajj, he did tawaf around the House and when he went to Safa he found Jibril there. Jibril said to him, 'O Allah's chosen one [Safiullah, صفي الله], unwrap your robe[76] when you reach the bottom of the wadi.' Musa wrapped his waist with his cloth, then when he reached the bottom of the wadi he walked fast while saying, *'at you service, O Allah, at your service.'*"

The narrator continued: "Allah the Almighty said, 'Here I Am, Musa; I Am with you.'"

92 - Uthman said, Sadiq informed me that it reached him that the messenger of Allah said:
"70 prophets have passed through the route of Rouhaa (or he said 'this route'); all of them were riding red camels that are bridled with palm fiber ropes and were wearing cloaks. They recited their Talbiyah in different ways. Amongst them was Younis ibn Matta,[77] who was saying, *'at your service, O You who relieve our hardships, at your service.'* And Musa was saying, *'at your service, I am your slave, at your service, at your service.'*"

The narrator continued: "and the Talbiyah of Isa[78] was, *'at your service, I am your slave, the son of your female slave, the daughter of your two slaves, at your service.'*"

93 - Uthman said, Muqatil informed me, saying:
"In the Sacred Mosque, between Zamzam and the Corner, there are the graves of 70 prophets, amongst them Hud, Saleh, and Ismail, while the graves of Adam, Ibrahim, Ishaak, Ya'kub, and Yousuf are in Bayt al-Maqdis."[79]

94 - My grandfather narrated to me, on the authority of Sa'id ibn Salim, on the authority of Uthman ibn Saj, on the authority of Wahb ibn Munabbih, who said, Salih addressed those who believed with him, saying to them:
"'The wrath of Allah is on this residence and its people, therefore you should leave it, for it is not your place.' They said, 'our choice is yours, so tell us what to do and we will obey.' He said, 'go to the Sanctuary of Allah and its safety; I cannot see any other place for you.' They immediately recited the Talbiyah to do Hajj, entered the state of Ihram wearing their cloaks, and rode red camels bridled with fiber ropes. They set off towards the Forbidden House. When they reached Mecca, they stayed there until they died. Their graves are at the western side of the Ka'ba, between the

---

76. Robes needed to be wrapped at the waist to run.
77. The parallel of Yona (Jonah) son of Amittai in the Hebrew Bible.
78. The Islamic parallel of Jesus.
79. Literally "the Holy House." This term is used to refer to Jerusalem and its surroundings.

house of al-Nadwa and the house of Bani-Hashim. The same thing was done by the prophet Hud and the believers of his people, and prophet Shoaib the believers of his people."

95 – My grandfather narrated to me, on the authority of a man of knowledge who said, Muhammad ibn Muslim Razi told him, on the authority of Jarir ibn 'Abdul Hamid Razi, on the authority of al-Fadl bin 'Atiya, on the authority Atta' ibn al-Sa'ib, who narrated:

"Ibrahim caught sight of a man performing tawaf around the House, and he did not know him. Ibrahim asked the man, 'who are you [or where are you from]?' The man said, 'from the companions of Dhul-Qarnain.' Ibrahim asked, 'where is he?' The man replied, 'he is there at al-Abtah.'[80] Ibrahim went there to meet him, and he embraced him. Dhul-Qarnain was asked, 'why do you not ride?' He replied, 'how could I ride while this man walks?' Therefore, he performed his Hajj walking."

The Ka'ba as the First House Established for Mankind

96 - Abu Muhammad narrated to us, saying, Abu al-Walid narrated to us, saying, my grandfather narrated to me, on the authority of Sa'id ibn Salim, on the authority of Uthman ibn Saj, who said, Ibn Jurayj informed me, saying:

"We have heard the Jews said, 'Bayt al-Maqdis is superior to the Ka'ba, because the prophets migrated to it, and because it is in the Holy Land.' The Muslims said, 'the Ka'ba is superior.' When the prophet Muhammad heard about this, this verse was revealed, '*the first House established for mankind was that at Bakka, full of blessing,*' until he recited, '*therein are clear signs: the station of Ibrahim,*' which is not in Bayt al-Maqdis [and] '*whosoever enters it shall be secure,*' which is not in Bayt al-Maqdis" (Qur'an 3:96-97).

Uthman said: "Khaseef told me, '*the first House established for mankind,*' he said, '[is] the first mosque established for mankind.'"

Mujahid said: "the first House established for mankind [is] like the saying, '*you are the best community brought forth unto mankind*'" (Qur'an 3:110).

97 - Uthman said, Muhammad ibn Abban informed me, on the authority of Zayd ibn Aslam:

"He read, '*the first House established for mankind*' until he reached, '*therein are clear signs: the station of Ibrahim;*' he said, 'the evident sign is the Maqam of Ibrahim; "*whosoever enters it shall be secure. Pilgrimage to the House is a duty upon mankind before God for those who can find a way,*"' and he said, '*they will come from all deep and distant mountain highways*'" (Qur'an 3:97; 22:27).

98 - Uthman said, Muhammad ibn Ishaq informed me that:

"The saying of Allah the Exalted, '*the first House established for mankind was that at Bakka,*' means mosque, '*full of a blessing and a guidance for the worlds*'" (Qur'an 3:96). He said, '*that thou mayest warn the Mother of Cities and those around it*'" (Qur'an 42:7).

---
80. A place between Mecca and Mina, الأبطح.

99 - Uthman said, Yahya ibn Abi Anisah informed me regarding the saying of Allah, the Exalted, *'the first House established for mankind was that at Bakka, full of blessing'* (Qur'an 3:96), saying:

"Allah the Almighty has called the position of the Ka'ba a House before the existence of the Ka'ba on earth. Houses were built before it, but Allah named it House, and He made it blessed, and a guidance for all people—a qibla for them."

Ibrahim Makes Supplication for the Believers; Allah Relocates Ta'if and a Syriac Inscription is Found in the Corner

100 - Abu al-Walid narrated to us, saying, my grandfather informed me, saying, Sa'id ibn Salim narrated to us, on the authority of Uthman ibn Saj, who said, Musa ibn Ubaydah al-Rabadhi informed me, on the authority of Muḥammad ibn Ka'b al-Qurazi, who said:

"Ibrahim made supplication for the believers and did not make any supplication for the unbelievers. Allah the Almighty said, *'whosoever disbelieves, I will grant him enjoyment for a while, then I will compel him toward the punishment of the Fire'*" (Qur'an 2:126).

Zaid ibn Aslum said: "Ibrahim asked Allah to grant this (safety and sustenance) to those who believed him, while the disbelievers will return to the Fire."

101 - Uthman said, Muḥammad ibn al-Sa'ib al-Kalbi informed me, saying:

"Ibrahim said, *'my Lord, make this a land secure, and provide its people with fruits: those among them who believe in God and the Last Day'* (Qur'an 2:126). Allah the Almighty answered his supplication and made it (Mecca) a safe land where frightened people could find protection, and its people were provided with fruits, carried to them from the heavens."

102 - Uthman said, Muqatil ibn Hayyan said:

"Ibrahim made his supplication of sustenance for the believers only. Then Allah the Almighty said, 'those who disbelieve, I will sustain (and nourish) them just like the believers, but it will be for a short time during their life in this world, then I will force them to the punishment of the Fire, a miserable destination.'"

103 – Uthman said, Mujahid said:

"Allah has made this land (Mecca) a safe place; no one who enters it feels afraid."

104 - My grandfather narrated to me, saying, Ibrahim ibn Muḥammad ibn al-Muntashir narrated to me, saying, Sa'id ibn al-Sa'ib ibn Yasar narrated to me, saying, I heard some of the descendants of Nafi' ibn Jubayr ibn Mut'im and others mention that they heard:

"When Ibrahim made his supplication for Mecca to provide its people with fruits, Allah the Almighty moved the land of Ta'if from the north and placed it there, to provide (or sustain) the Sanctuary."

105 - My grandfather narrated to me, saying, Ibrahim ibn Muḥammad narrated to us, on the authority of Muḥammad ibn al-Munkadir, on the authority of the prophet who said:

"When Allah placed the Sanctuary, He moved al-Ta'if to it from the north."

106 - Mahdi ibn Abi al-Mahdi narrated to me, saying, Yahya ibn Salim narrated to us, saying, I heard Abdul Rahman ibn Nafi' ibn Jubayr ibn Mut'im say, I heard al-Zuhri say:

"Allah the Almighty has moved a town from the north and placed it at al-Ta'if, to answer the supplication of Ibrahim Khalilullah who said, *'and provide its people with fruits.'*"

> In Islamic history, the location of Ta'if is associated with Mecca. While the Qur'ān does not mention Ta'if by name, it is thought that the 'two towns' of Surah 43:31 are Mecca and Ta'if. According to the hadith, the prophet Muḥammad would preach in Ta'if when he was near Mecca. Yāqūt tells us that it was a three-day journey to get from one to the other.
>
> Startingly, Azraqi describes Ta'if being moved from the north of Arabia to the south. Could it be that when the Holy City of Islam was moved from Petra to the Hijaz that the people of the former Ta'if, a village three day's journey from Petra, also relocated to the Hijaz and founded a village there by the same name?

107 - My grandfather narrated to me, saying, Muslim ibn Khalid al-Zanji narrated to us, on the authority of Ibn Jurayj, on the authority of Kathir ibn Kathir, on the authority of Sa'id ibn Jubayr, on the authority of Ibn Abbas, who said:

"Ibrahim came to visit Ismail, but he did not find him. [Ibrahim] found his second wife al-Saiyda bint Madhadh ibn Amr al-Jurhumi. Ibrahim greeted her and she replied nicely and asked him to stay for some time with them and offered him food and drink. Ibrahim said, 'what is your food and drink?' She replied, 'meat and water.' He said, 'do you have grains or any other food?' She said, 'no.' Ibrahim said, 'may Allah bless your food and your drink.'"

Ibn Abbas said: "the prophet said, 'if at that day he (Ibrahim) had found any grains in Ismail's house, he would have prayed to Allah to bless their grains, and that land would have become a cultivated land.'"

Sa'id ibn al-Jubayr said: "if anyone eats only meat and water in any place other than Mecca, he will have a stomachache. And if he eats them in Mecca, he will not have any pain."

Sa'id ibn Salem said: "I am not sure whether Ibn Abbas told Sa'id ibn al-Jubayr that narration or not, referring to eating meat and water in and outside Mecca."

108 - My grandfather narrated to me, saying, Muslim ibn Khalid narrated to us, on the authority of Abdullah ibn Abdul Rahman ibn Abi Husayn, on the authority of Ibn Abbas, who said:

"A book was found in the Maqam [that read], 'this is the Forbidden House of Allah in Mecca. Allah guarantees that He will give provision to its people from three [sources]. Their water, meat, and milk are blessed. Its sacredness will not be desecrated by the first (generations) of its people.' A text which was created out of stones was found in a stone in al-Hijr [that read], 'I Am Allah, the Master of the Sacred Bakka; I [positioned] it on the day I created the sun and the moon, and made it surrounded by seven angels whose faith is pure to Allah. It will not come to an end until the Akhshaban[81] come to an end. My blessings will be on its meat and water.'"

109 - My grandfather narrated to me, saying, Ibrahim ibn Muḥammad narrated to us, saying, Rashid ibn Kurayb narrated to us, on the authority of his father, on the authority of Ibn Abbas, who said:
"When the Ka'ba was demolished and they reached to the foundation of Ibrahim, they found a text in one of the foundation stones. They called for a man from al-Yemen and another man who was a monk. The writing read, 'I Am Allah, the Master of Bakka; I made it sacred on the day I created the heavens, the earth, the sun, and the moon, and on the day I created those two mountains. I made it surrounded by seven angels whose faith is pure to Allah.'"

110 - My grandfather narrated to me, on the authority of Sa'id ibn Salim, on the authority of Uthman ibn Saj, who said, Ibn Jurayj informed me, saying, Mujahid informed us, saying:
"in a stone in the Hijr: 'I Am Allah the Master of Bakka; I shaped it on the day I shaped the sun and the moon and made it surrounded by seven angels whose faith is pure to Allah. Its meat and water are blessed. Its people will desecrate its sacredness, and it would not be desecrated by the first generations.'"

The narrator continued: "it will not come to an end until the Akhshaban come to an end."

Abu Muḥammad al-Khuza'i said: "al-Akhshaban means the two mountains."

111 - My grandfather narrated to me, on the authority of Sa'id ibn Salim, on the authority of Uthman ibn Saj, who said, Khasif ibn Abdul Rahman informed me, on the authority of Mujahid, who said:
"It has been found in some copies of the Zabur,[82] 'I Am Allah, the Master of Becca. I made it between these two mountains, and I formed it on the day I formed the sun and the moon and made it surrounded by seven angels of the Hanafa'.[83] Its people will have their provision from three paths.[84] The people of Mecca cannot come except through the three paths, from the top of the wadi to the bottom. So therefore I blessed her family with meat and water.'"

112 - My grandfather narrated to me, saying, Sa'id ibn Salim narrated to us, on the authority of Uthman, who said, Muḥammad ibn Ishaq informed me, saying, Yahya ibn 'Abbad ibn Abdullah ibn al-Zubayr narrated to us, on the authority of his father, 'Abbad, that he narrated to him:
"Two books have been found in the ruined bottom of the well of the Ka'ba, slightly yellow like ostrich eggs. One of them said, 'this is the Forbidden House of Allah.

---

81. Two mountains in Mecca, الأخشبان.
82. Muslim parallel of the Psalms of David.
83. "Angels of the Hanafa'" could refer to angels that are watching over those who follow the Hanafiyyah faith.
84. There are indeed three paths that lead from the hills overlooking Petra, down through the Petra valley and into Wadi Araba below.

Allah has granted (the virtue of) worship to its people. Its sacredness will not be desecrated by the first (generations) of its people.' The other book revealed a declaration of immunity to the sons of an unnamed people (a branch of an Arab tribe) for performing pilgrimage for the sake of Allah."

113 - My grandfather narrated to me, saying, Uthman said, Ibn Ishaq informed me:
"The tribe of Quraysh found a book in the Corner, written in a Syriac language. They did not know what it said until a Jewish man came and read it for them. He said, 'it says, "I Am Allah the Master of Bakka, I created it on the day I created the heavens and the earth and when I shaped the sun and the moon. I made it surrounded by seven angels whose faith is pure to Allah. It will not come to an end until its Akhshaban come to an end. Its water and milk are blessed."'"

114 - My grandfather narrated to me, saying, Uthman said, Muḥammad ibn Ishaq informed me, saying:
"Layth ibn Abi Saleem claims that they found a stone in the Ka'ba 40 pilgrimages (years) before the prophet had been sent as an Apostle—that is the year of the Elephant [al-Feel]. If what he said is true, [it read], 'whoever plants goodness, he will harvest happiness. And whoever plants badness, he will harvest regret. You do evil deeds and [hope to be] rewarded good deeds, indeed, like grapes that cannot be harvested from thorns.'"

The Descendants of Ismail and the Destruction of the Amalekites and the Jurhum

115 - Abu al-Walid narrated to us, saying, Mahdi ibn Abi al-Mahdi narrated to us, saying, Abdullah ibn Ma'adh al-San'ani narrated to us, on the authority of Ma'mar, on the authority of Qatadah, that Umar ibn al-Khattab said to the Quraysh:
"This House was ruled by (the tribe of) Tasam, who underestimated its worth and desecrated its sacredness, thus Allah the Almighty destroyed them. After them (the tribe of) Jurhum ruled the House. They underestimated its worth and desecrated its sacredness, thus Allah the Almighty destroyed them. Therefore, do not devalue the House, but revere its sacredness."

116 - My grandfather narrated to me, saying, Sa'id ibn Salim narrated to us, on the authority of Uthman ibn Saj, who said, Ibn Ishaq informed me, saying:
"Ismail, the son of Ibrahim, was a father to 12 men; their mother was al-Saiyda bint Madhadh ibn Amr al-Jurhumi. She gave birth to 12 men: Nabit ibn Ismail, Kaydar ibn Ismail, Wasil ibn Ismail, Mayas ibn Ismail, Azer and Tima ibn Ismail, Yatour ibn Ismail, Nabash ibn Ismail, and Kaidama ibn Ismail. It is mentioned that Ismail lived for one hundred and thirty years. Allah has spread the Arabs from the offspring of Nabit ibn Ismail and Kaydar ibn Ismail. Kaidar and Nabit were the oldest of Ismail's sons. It has been said by the Jurhum and the children of Ismail

that when Ismail died, he was buried next to his mother in al-Hijr. They claimed that she was buried there when she died.

"Nabit ibn Ismail was assigned as the ruler of the House for as long as Allah willed, then after Nabit had died, the House was ruled by Madhadh ibn Amr al-Jurhumi, who was Nabit's grandfather from his mother's side. He gathered the children of Nabit ibn Ismail and the children of Ismail under his rule. They stayed with their grandfather from their mother's side, Madhadh ibn Amr al-Jurhumi, and with their maternal family from Jurhum. The people of Mecca at that time were Jurhum and Qedar. The king of Jurhum was Madhadh ibn Amr, and the king of Qedar a man called al-Samaida'. When they departed al-Yemen they came walking on foot, and they did not leave al-Yemen before appointing a king over them. When they reached Mecca, they found it a good place that had water and trees and they liked it; therefore, they decided to stay there.

"Madhadh ibn Amr and those who were with him from Jurhum stayed at the upper part of Mecca and Qaiqa'an, and he ruled over it. On the other hand, al-Samaida' stayed at Ajyadeen and the lower part of Mecca. Madhadh ibn Amr received tithes (sums of money paid) from the people entering Mecca from the upper side, and al-Samaida' received tithes from the people entering Mecca from the lower side and from Kadda. Each one of them was staying with his people without interfering with the other. After a while, Jurhum and Qedar transgressed against each other and each side competed for the sovereignty of Mecca, which led to a war between them.

"The rulers of Mecca, the sons of Nabit ibn Ismail and the sons of Ismail, were with Madhadh ibn Amr. Governing the House was assigned to Amr, not to al-Samaida'. The transgression continued between the two sides until they faced each other on land. Madhadh ibn Amr went out from Qaiqa'an with a battalion, walking towards al-Samaida'. The battalion was armed with spears, leather shields, swords, and quivers, clanging loudly. It is said that Qaiqa'an [which means loud sound of metal objects] was named after this day. In Qedar, al-Samaida' advanced from Ajyad with men and horses. It is said the Ajyad was named because of the strong horses [jiyad] that came out from this place with al-Samaida'. The two sides met at (a place called) Fadih and they battled brutally until al-Samaida' was killed and Qedar was defeated. It is said that Fadih was named because of that incident. After that, the two sides agreed to reconcile, so they went to (a place called) al-Matabikh in a valley in the upper part of Mecca. [It was] called the valley of Abdullah ibn Aamir ibn Kareez ibn Rabia' ibn Habib ibn Abd-Shams. They reconciled there and submitted to the leadership to Madhadh ibn Amr al-Jurhumi. When he became the leader of all the people in Mecca and was chosen a king, Amr slaughtered (animals) to feed the people of Mecca and they cooked the food there for everyone. It is said the place was named al-Matabikh ['the kitchens'] for that reason."

The narrator continued: "it is claimed that what happened between Madhadh ibn Amr and al-Samaida' was the first transgression in Mecca, and Madhadh ibn Amr al-Jurhumi said, 'that is war,' mentioning al-Samaida', his death, his transgression, and his quest to take what did not belong to him:

We killed the master of that area deliberately,
and made him regret what he did.
Ruling this place is a right to us only,
and we are the legitimate kings, not al-Samaida'.
When he tried to take over our right to rule,
he was brutally defeated.
We constructed the House and we are the rulers,
defending it against any transgression.
Only we deserve the honor of ruling this place,
and our ancestors were kings in the old days,
and we inherited great kingdoms that cannot be defeated easily."

Ibn Ishaq said: "some scholars have claimed that the place was called al-Matabikh when Tubba' cooked for people there, and it was his place of residence."

The narrator continued: "then Allah the Almighty made the sons of Ismail spread out in Mecca, at the time when the maternal uncles of the Jurhum were the rulers of Mecca and the guardians of the House. They did that after the death of Nabit ibn Ismail. When Mecca became crowded with its people, they spread out around the earth looking for places to live and settle. Among all the places and the peoples they visited, Allah the Almighty made them the superior ones because of their religion, until they ruled over all the lands they reached. They banished the Amalekites and whoever was in their lands. The Jurhum continued to rule Mecca and guard the House, with no interference from the sons of Ismail, because of their maternal ties of kinship, and because they revered the Sanctuary [Haram] and avoided any transgression or fight in it."

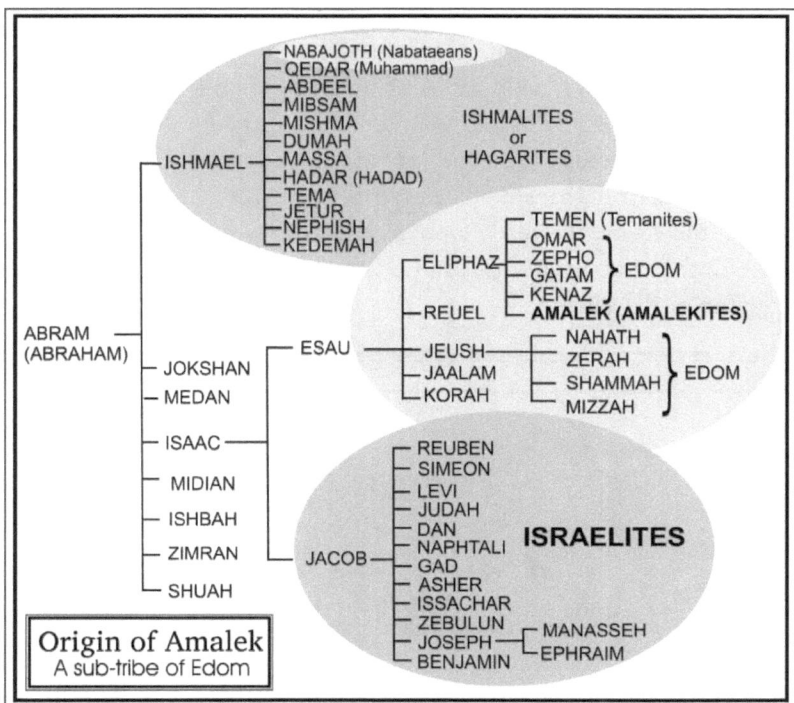

Origin of Amalek
A sub-tribe of Edom

117 - Some scholars reported:

"The Amalekites were the rulers of Mecca until they lost reverence for the Forbidden House, and they made lawful what was unlawful for them, and committed grievous sins. Then a man called Amlouq said to them, 'oh people, do not destroy yourselves. You have seen and heard how the former nations of Hud and Saleh and Shoaib perished. So do not do the same and lose your reverence for the sanctuary of Allah and His House. And beware committing oppression and atheism in the House, as no one who has settled here has committed oppression and atheism without being rooted out and destroyed by Allah—removed from this land until no one is left.' The people of Amalek did not accept what the man told them, and they kept doing their evil deeds.

"It has been said that Jurhum and Qedar came out from Yemen walking on foot, as their land became bare and dry. They traveled with their children, animals, and money and they said, 'we are looking for a place where our animals can graze and where, if we like it, we can settle in it. Any land where one can settle with their children and money becomes their homeland; otherwise, we will go back to our land.' When they arrived at Mecca, they found good water, great trees called Salam and Samar, and grass that could nourish their animals. It was a vast land, with warmth against the cold of winter. They said, 'this place has all the things we need,' and they stayed there with the Amalekites.

"It was a tradition among the people of Yemen to pick a leader for themselves when they were traveling, even if their numbers were small, in order to take care of all their matters. Al-Madhadh ibn Amr became the leader of the Jurhum, and everyone obeyed him. Al-Samaida' was the leader of the Qedar in the same way. Madhadh ibn Amr stayed at the upper side of Mecca and received tithes from people entering Mecca from that side. Their territory (or areas they controlled) was the front side of the Ka'ba, the Black Corner, al-Maqam, the place of Zamzam, and from there all the areas on the right and on the left side—going up to al-Qaiqa'an and to the top of the valley.

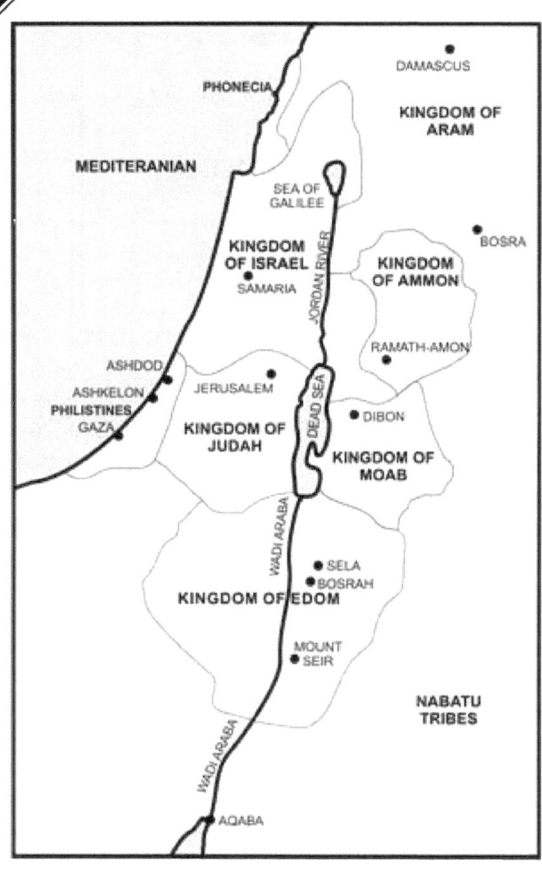

The Amalekites (عماليق) were the descendants of Amalek and were related by blood to the other Edomite tribes (Genesis 36:12, 16). Amalek was the eldest son of Eliphaz, Eliphaz the eldest son of Esau, Esau and eldest son of Isaac, and Isaac was the second son of Abraham. Because of Amalek's importance in Esau's line, Amalek was counted among the chiefs of Edom, and many Edomites were referred to as Amalekites. This broad use of "Amalekite" is similar to how the term "Nabataean" could refer to all of the tribes of Ishmael when they cooperated with each other.

Amalek's mother was Eliphaz's concubine Timna. Timna was the daughter of Seir the Horite, after whom the mountains of Seir were named. Eventually the city of Petra would be built at Mount Seir.

Azraqi indicates above that God sent the prophet Amlouq to the Amalekites to warn them against "committing oppression and atheism in the House" when they controlled the Ka'ba.

> According to Exodus 17:8, the Amalekites were the first enemies to challenge Israel after Israel crossed the Red Sea. The last surviving Amalekites seem to have been destroyed during the reign of Hezekiah of Judah when 500 sons of Simeon attacked them in the mountains of Seir near modern day Petra (I Chronicles 4:43).
>
> When these traditions are considered as a whole, the history of Amalek provides an important historical connection between Seir and the Ka'ba—textual evidence which agrees with the archaeological evidence that Petra (Mount Seir) was the original Holy City of Islam.

"Al-Samaida' stayed in the lower part of Mecca and Ajyadeen, and he received tithes from people who entered Mecca from the lower side. Their borders were al-Masfala, the back side of the Ka'ba, the Yemeni Corner, the Western Corner, Ajyadeen, and al-Thanya to al-Ramdha. They (al-Madhadh and al-Samaida') built many houses over a large area and eventually they outnumbered the Amalekites, who started disputing with them, but were prevented by the Jurhum. After that the Jurhum banished the Amalekites to outside of the Haram area and they stayed at the outer corners of it and were not allowed to enter it again. The man named Amlouq said to them, 'didn't I tell you not to lose the reverence of the sanctuary? But you ignored me.'

"Al-Madhadh and al-Samaida' started to grant houses to whoever came to them from their people. They became great in number and they liked the place. They were Arab people, speaking the Arabic language. When Ibrahim Khalilullah visited Ismail, he listened to their speech and rhetoric. He heard a good language and observed the Arab people. Ismail at that time had learned their language and was speaking like them. Ibrahim ordered Ismail to marry a woman from them, so he proposed to the daughter of Madhadh ibn Amr who was named Ra'la, and he married her. She gave birth to ten male children and was the mother of the house and Ismail's wife. She washed Ibrahim's head when he put his foot on the Maqam. It has been said that when Ismail died he was buried at al-Hijr where his mother was buried as well. He left children behind with their mother Ra'la bint Madhadh ibn Amr al-Jurhumi. After the death of Ismail, Madhadh supported Ismail's children and was responsible for them, as they were his daughter's children. The tribe of Jurhum continued to grow and greaten its presence in Mecca until they became the rulers of the House and the rulers of all of Mecca. When a flood came into Mecca and entered the House and caused it to collapse, the Jurhum rebuilt the House in the same way that Ibrahim did. The House was nine cubits tall."

Some scholars said: "the one who rebuilt the House for Jurhum was a man called Abu al-Jadrah; he was known as Amr al-Jadir, and his people were named the Bani al-Jadrah."

The narrator continued: "later, the Jurhum lost their reverence for the sanctuary and committed great sins that had never been done before. Al-Madhadh ibn Amr ibn al-Harith stood up and said to them, 'oh people, beware of the transgression, as no one will survive if you keep doing them. You have seen what has happened to the Amalekites: they lost the sanctuary of the Haram and did not exalt it. They disputed and differed among themselves until Allah gave you power over them, and you banished them outside the Haram and caused them to disperse. Therefore, do not depreciate the sanctuary of Allah's House and do not oppress those who come to visit it, glorifying its sacredness, or those who come to sell their goods or desire to be your neighbors, for if you do I am afraid that you will be banished outside it in a humiliating way until you will be unable to reach the Haram or visit the House. [It] is a safe a secured place for you where even the birds find safety in it.'

"One of them (from Jurhum) named Mujdi' stood up and said, 'who can get us out of this place? Aren't we the most powerful and righteous among Arabs? We are the ones with the greatest numbers of men!' Madhadh ibn Amr said, 'if the command has come (from Allah) then what you said is abolished.' But they did not stop their sinful deeds. There was a well inside the Ka'ba where they stored jewels and valuable objects that were gifted to the House. At that time, the House was roofless, so five men from the Jurhum planned to steal what was inside the well. On each of the House's Corners stood a man from those five and the fifth man broke into the Ka'ba. Allah the Almighty made him fall upside down into the well and die, while the other four ran away. After this, (the act of) wiping over the four Corners started. It is said that Ibrahim Khalilullah also wiped over the four Corners, and before him Adam did.

"After the attempt to steal what was inside the well of the Ka'ba by the five men, Allah the Almighty sent a snake that had a black back and a white abdomen; its head looked like a goat's head. It guarded the House for five hundred years. No one committed evil at the House without being ruined by Allah the Almighty, and no one dared to steal what was inside the Ka'ba. When the Quraysh wanted to rebuild the Ka'ba, they were prevented by the snake. Then they stayed at the Maqam, praying to Allah, and saying, 'oh Allah, we only wanted to build Your House.' Later, a bird came; it had a black back, white front, and yellow feet. The bird took the snake and carried it to Ajyad."

Some scholars said: "when the Jurhum did their sinful deeds in the Haram, a man called Isaf and a woman called Nai'la entered the House and committed an act of obscenity inside it. Allah the Almighty caused them to turn into two rocks. Then they were brought out of the Ka'ba and were erected on Safa and Marwa so people could be admonished when they saw them and were warned not to do the same act. It continued like that until, with time, people started worshipping them."

Some scholars said: "the first to call for people to worship those two rocks was Amr ibn Luhi, and he said, 'those idols were erected here because your fathers and those who were before you were worshipping them.' This was an act of Iblis. Amr ibn Luhi was a noble person to whom people listened. Whatever he said was followed like a religion by people."

The narrator continued: "later, the two rocks were moved by Qusai ibn Kilab into the area facing the Ka'ba near Zamzam, and he slaughtered (animals) in front of them."

[Azraqi adds]: "their lineage was not confirmed to us. Some said, 'the man was called Isaf ibn Bagha, and the woman was called Nai'la bint Thi'b.' What is established [comes] to us from [he] who we trust, Abdul Rahman ibn Abi-Zinad, who said, 'the man is Isaf ibn Suhail, and the woman is Nai'la bint Amr ibn Theeb.'"

Some scholars said: "the man did not have intercourse with her in the House, but he kissed her."

They (the scholars) said: "they remained to be worshipped until the Day of Conquest [Fatih] when they were broken. Mecca was a place where no oppressor or dissolute or transgressor came without being exiled from it. At the time of the Amalekites and the Jurhum some tyrants settled in Mecca. Whoever intended to harm the House with evil acts, Allah destroyed. For that reason (Mecca) was called al-Bassah."[85]

118 - It has been narrated on the authority of Abdullah ibn Amr ibn al-A'as that:
"It was called Bakka because it breaks[86] the tyrants' necks."

119 - My grandfather narrated to me, saying:
"It was called al-Bayt al-Ateeq because it was spared[87] from the tyrants' control."

120 - It is narrated from Ata ibn Yasar and Muḥammad ibn Ka'b al-Qurazi that they used to say:
"It was called al-Bayt al-Ateeq because it is ancient."

121 - My grandfather and Ibrahim ibn Muḥammad al-Shafi'i narrated to me, saying, Muslim ibn Khalid al-Zanji narrated to us, on the authority of Ibn Khuthaym, who said:
"There was a group of people living in Mecca called the Amalekites. They caused a lot of corruption and trouble. Allah the Almighty sent them rainfalls (in distant locations to draw them out of Mecca); they kept following the rainfalls from place to place but they could not reach them, until they reached the hometown of their fathers, who were originally from Himyar. After that Allah the Almighty sent al-Tofan to them."

Abu Khalid al-Zinji said: "I asked Ibn Khuthaym, 'what is al-Tofan?' He said, 'it is death.'"

---

85. Meaning the destroyer, الباسة.
86. Pronounced in Arabic as Tabuk, تَبُك.
87. Pronounced in Arabic Otika, عَتَق.

122 - My grandfather narrated to me, on the authority of Sa'id ibn Salim, on the authority of Uthman ibn Saj, who said, Talhah ibn Amr al-Hadrami informed me, on the authority of Ata, on the authority of Ibn Abbas:

"There was a group called Amalekites in Mecca; their number was large, and they were very wealthy and strong. They had many horses, camels, and livestock, which were grazing on Mur and Numan[88] in and around Mecca. They enjoyed shady and cool autumns, fruitful springs, valleys covered with grass, big twisted trees, and lush meadows. They were living in prosperity, but they transgressed and sinned greatly against themselves, and they did acts of disobedience and oppressed whoever came near them. They did not thank Allah for all the blessings He gave them until He (Allah) took everything away from them. He did not send them rain and their land became dry. They used to rent the shady places in Mecca and sell the water; then Allah the Almighty punished them with armies of small ants which overpowered them and sent them out of the Haram, and they stayed around it. Then Allah dragged them out of Mecca by making their lands dry and sending rainfalls in areas in front of them. They followed the rainfalls from [one] place to another, but they were never able to reach them, until they reached the hometowns of their fathers. They were Arabs from Himyar and when they entered al-Yemen they were scattered around and ruined. Allah the Almighty replaced them with the Jurhum, who settled in the Haram after the Amalekites. They dwelled there until they started transgressing and lost their sense of responsibility towards the Haram; then Allah ruined them all as well."

The Khuza'i Destroy the Jurhum and Rule Mecca for 500 Years; the Khuza'i Change the Hanifiyyah

123 - Abu al-Walid narrated to us, saying, my grandfather narrated to me, saying, Sa'id ibn Salim narrated to us, on the authority of Uthman ibn Saj, on the authority of al-Kalbi, on the authority of Abu Salih, who said:

"When the Jurhum's period of rule lasted for a long time, they started committing unlawful things and they ignored the sanctity of the Haram. They used the money that was gifted to the Ka'ba secretly and publicly. The acts of the abusive and vulgar ones were defended by the noble men. They oppressed whoever entered Mecca who were outsiders. Then one day a man entered the Ka'ba with a woman. Some say they had intercourse and others say they kissed each other. They were transformed into two rocks. From then on, the condition of the Jurhum weakened; they became divided and they disputed and disagreed over many problems, even though they were one of the strongest tribes among the Arabs—[the tribe] with the largest number of men, weapons, and money.

"When a man from them called Madhadh ibn Amr ibn Harith ibn Madhadh ibn Amr saw what was happening to his tribe, he said admonishing them, 'oh people, save yourselves, and beware Allah and protect His sanctuary, and be thankful

---

88. Names of plants.

for the safety that He gave you. You have seen how the early generations of this nation had ruined: the people of Hud, Saleh, and Shoaib, so do not do the same. Advocate what is moral and forbid what is immoral, and do not belittle the sanctity of Allah's Haram and His Forbidden House. Beware of committing oppression and atheism in the House, as this will be a great loss. You know that no one has settled here committing oppression and atheism without being rooted out and destroyed by Allah and removed from this land. Beware of transgressions, as they will destroy you. You have seen and heard about the people who have lived here before you, people from Tasam, Jadees, and the Amalekites, who were longer lived and were stronger than you. They had more men, money, and children, but when they transgressed and belittled the sanctity of the Haram, Allah evicted them from the Haram in various ways. Some were evicted by the small ants, some moved out because of the dry land, and some by the power of swords. You have lived in their places, and inherited the lands after them, so praise and respect the sanctuary of Allah and honor His Forbidden House and do not oppress those who come to glorify its sacredness, or those who come to sell their goods in it or to live near you. If you do, I am worried that you will be evicted from the sanctuary of Allah in a humiliating way until you will be unable to reach the Haram or visit the Forbidden House which was once a safe place for you, and is still a safe place even for the birds and the beasts.'

"One man from the Jurhum, his name was Mujdi', stood up to reply to what was said by Madhadh. He said, 'who can evict us from here? Aren't we the strongest of Arabs? We have the largest numbers of men and weapons!'

"Madhadh ibn Amr said to him, 'if the command comes (from Allah), what you said is abolished.' They did not stop their sinful deeds, and when Madhadh ibn Amr ibn al-Harith saw what the Jurhum were doing in the Haram, and what they are stealing from the treasure of Ka'ba in secret and in public, he went to the Ka'ba and took two (statues of) gazelles made out of gold, and some precious swords, and he buried them in the place of Zamzam's well. By that time the water of Zamzam had disappeared as a result of the bad acts that the Jurhum were doing in the Haram. The location of the well of Zamzam was completely hidden from view. One dark night al-Madhadh and some of his sons dug a deep hole in the place of Zamzam and buried the swords and the two golden gazelles there.

"The situation continued like that in Mecca, while in Yemen [Ma'rib] a fortune teller called Tarifah predicted the future for Amr ibn Aamer, who was named Maziqya' ibn Ma' As-Sama'. His full name was Amr ibn Aamer ibn Haritha ibn Tha'laba ibn Imro'-Alqais ibn Mazin ibn al-Azd ibn al-Ghouth ibn Nabat ibn Malik ibn Zaid ibn Kahlan ibn Saba' ibn Yashjub ibn Ya'rib ibn Qahtan. The fortune teller saw in her predictions that the dam of Ma'rib would collapse and that the flood of Arim would destroy the two flourishing gardens. Accordingly, Amr ibn Aamer sold everything he had and moved away with his people from place to place.

Every place they visited, they overpowered the people who inhabited the place until they moved out to another place."

[Azraqi comments]: "this has a very long story, but it is shortened here."

The narrator continued: "when they came closer to Mecca, the fortune-teller Tarifah said to them, 'walk ahead, walk ahead, you will not ever be reunited with those who you left behind. This is a root for you, and you are a branch from it.' Then she said, 'Ma ma,[89] I say nothing except the wisdom of the Wise, Lord of all peoples, Arabs, and foreigners.' They said to her, 'what is wrong with you Tarifah?' She said, 'take the animals and smear them with blood, then you will dwell in the land of Jurhum, the neighbors of the Forbidden House.'

The narrator continued: "Mecca was at that time ruled by Jurhum, who overpowered many people and governed the house instead of the sons of Ismail. When the people of Ma'rib reached Mecca, a man called Tha'labah ibn Amr ibn Aamer sent (a message) to Jurhum saying, 'oh people, we have left our country and in any place we stay we overpower its people. They allow us to reside with them until we send out our scouts; [our scouts] come back to us after finding new places where we can live. Therefore, allow us to stay in your land until we rest and send our scouts to al-Sham and the east. Then we will go to whichever suits us best. I hope that our stay with you will not be for a long time.' Jurhum strongly refused their request and said, 'we don't want you to stay with us, as you will make our land crowded and you will share our resources, so leave our land and go wherever you like; we do not need you near.' Tha'labah sent another message to Jurhum saying, 'we have no other choice but to stay in this land for a year until the messengers I sent come back to us. Therefore, if you willingly allow me to stay, I will thank you and will respectfully share the water and the grazing land with you. But if you refuse, I will stay forcibly, and then you will only reach the grazing land when I allow you, and you will only drink al-Ranq.'

"Abu al-Walid was asked, 'what is al-Ranq?' He responded, 'it is dirty [or cloudy] water. Now I recite to you from Zuhayr:

It is like her saliva upon awakening,
like what was left of the perfume.
Water flowed down to her palms,
water soft and free of minerals,
water not cloudy.
So if you kill me, I will kill all of you.
If I come upon you,
I will capture your women and kill your men.
I will not leave one of you to come near the Haram.'

"Jurhum again refused Tha'labah's request to stay near them and they prepared to fight him. They battled for three days which ended with the defeat of Jurhum.

---

89. "Ma ma" may be an ancient idiomatic expression. Its meaning is unclear.

No one of them survived. Al-Madhadh ibn Amr ibn al-Harith had left Jurhum by that time and he did not support them in that war. He said, 'I had warned you of this.' He moved away with his sons and his family and settled in Kanuna and Hali and the surrounding area. The remnants of Jurhum are still there to this day.

"The tribe of Jurhum perished in that war, and Mecca and its surroundings were inhabited for one year by Tha'labah, his people, and his army. While they were there, they suffered from fever, and they did not know what the fever was. They called Tarifah (the fortune-teller) and told her what had happened to them. She said, 'I have suffered from what you have told me as well, and this calamity will cause us to scatter.' They asked, 'what are you ordering us to do?' She replied, 'the prince is amongst you, and I can only facilitate.' They asked, 'what are you advising us to do?' She responded, 'those of you who can endure long distance, have a strong camel, and have new travel equipment should go to the great castle of Oman.' That was how the Azd Oman tribe originated. Then she said, 'those of you who are tough and can endure long-suffering should go to the Arak [or great trees] at the middle of Mur.' That was how the Khuza'i [tribe] originated. Then she said, 'those who want the (trees) fixed in the mud which feed people[90] should go to Yathrib.'[91] That was how the Aous and Khazraj [tribes] originated. She said, 'those of you who want liquors and sovereignty, and want to wear silk and brocade, should go to Basra and A'weer, which are part of the land of Sham, and were inhabited by the people of Jafnah from Ghassan.' Lastly, she said, 'those who want to wear light clothes, ride noble horses, enjoy treasures and provisions, and shed blood, they should go to the land of Iraq.' It was inhabited by the people of Jadhima al-Abrush, and those of the people of Ghassan who were in al-Heira, and the people of Mahraq.

"When their messengers came back, they divided into two groups. One group went to Oman, and they are the Azd of Oman. The other group led by Tha'labah ibn Amr ibn Aamer went towards al-Sham. The two sons of Harith ibn Tha'labah ibn Amr ibn Aamer, who are the Aous and Khazraj, settled in al-Medina; they became the Ansar. The people of Ghassan continued their way to al-Sham."

[Azraqi comments]: "this is a very long story, but it is shortened here."

[The narrator continued]: "The Khuza'i stayed in Mecca, and those who stayed there are the people of Rabia'a ibn Haritha ibn Amr ibn Aamer. He was known as Luhi; he became the ruler of Mecca and was responsible for serving at the Ka'ba. Hassan ibn Thabit al-Ansari composed a poem describing the settlement of the Khuza'i in Mecca, Aous and Khazraj in al-Medina, and Ghassan in al-Sham."

The narrator continued: "when the Khuza'i ruled Mecca and they became its people, the sons of Ismail came to them. [The sons of Ismail] did not take part in the war between Khuza'i and Jurhum. They asked for permission to live in and around Mecca. The Khuza'i approved and allowed them to stay. At that time, al-Madhadh

---

90. Likely palm trees.
91. Later called Medina.

ibn Amr ibn al-Harith was yearning to go back to Mecca and feeling very nostalgic. He sent to the Khuza'i asking permission to live there and be their neighbor. He explained how he was advising his people not to start a war against the Khuza'i and that they would not commit sins in the Haram. The Khuza'i refused and did not allow them to come back to al-Haram or live near them.

"Amr ibn Luhi (who is Rabia'a ibn Harithah ibn Amr ibn Aamer) said to his people, 'if anyone from Jurhum comes near the Haram, his blood is permissible.'

"One day, some camels that belonged to Madhadh ibn Amr ibn al-Harith ibn Madhadh ibn Amr al-Jurhumi went astray from Kanuna and headed to Mecca. He tracked the camels' trail until he found it leading towards Mecca. He traveled to the mountains from the side of Ajyad until he reached (the mount of) Aba Kobais to look for his camels at the bottom of the valley of Mecca. When he arrived there, he saw his camels being slaughtered and eaten, unable to reach them. He was afraid that if he went down into the valley he would be killed. Therefore, he went back to his people and composed a poem (describing how the conditions of his people had changed from being the rulers of Mecca and the most powerful in the region to being outcasts and weak):

As if the pilgrims to al-Safa and Anis were not evident
and as though Samir did not converse in the evening in Mecca,
and he did not sit cross-legged or was a mediator,
and the place where you bow down to Dhu-l Arakah is present.
Indeed, we were its people,
so we removed the adversities of the night,
and the ancient pitfalls,
and we replaced it, my lord, with a house of sojourn,
in which the wolf howls and the enemy is besieged.
If the whole world becomes annoyed with us
and becomes a situation after us and quarrels,
then we are the guardians of the house.
Carrying on in the tradition of Nabat
we roam this house.
Goodness became evident in our kingdom,
so we strengthened it,
and it is created in our kingdom,
so there is none living other than us.
Then my grandfather became proud
and married the best person he knew of.
His sons are among us and we are the in-laws.
If the world bends over us in its condition, then it has a state,
and there is quarreling in it.
So, we brought out the king from it with power.

*Thus, between people, destinies flow.
I say, if the husband sleeps and I do not sleep,
then the Throne will not remain level and firm,
and I exchanged their pride that I did not like,
and the donkeys I changed to lions,
and we started to talk about it and we were happy.
Likewise, the bygone years bit us, and tears of the eyes were shed,
crying for a town that has a safe sanctuary
and that has fond feelings in the valley of Anis
that does not harm a dove or repel it for a day
and has birds, and wild animals that do not trample—in Anis.
If we leave the valley,
I hope my poetry would stand firm in excellence.*

*So he went on his way,
to the outer area near the lower parts of Mina.
A wild animal was not pleased with him,
and from my love is the guidance of 'Amayar.
And he said, oh you who live, walk on.
Your shortcoming is that one day you will not walk with us.
We are as you were, and we will be different for an eternity.
You will become us, as we have become.
Urge the riding animal and relax from any crisis before death,
and fulfill what you decree for us.
An eternity has passed over us;
then we were destroyed by transgression in it
and people's righteousness forgot us.
Indeed, contemplation is of no use to the one
who does it with intuition and knowledge of his inferiority.
Decide your affairs with firmness.
Indeed, there are matters of soundness.
You have attained soundness.
Be strengthened, and inquire into the actions of the people before you,
just as the path of humility has become clear to them.
We were in the past.
The kings of people before you lived in inhabited dwellings
in the forbidden place* [haram] *of God.*

"Madhadh ibn Amr al-Jurhumi went towards al-Yaman with his people. They told stories about how they used to live in Mecca and what happened to them and how things changed. They became sad and they wept for Mecca, reciting poetry in praise and remembrance of their time there.

"The Khuza'i ruled Mecca and served at the Ka'ba. The sons of Ismail ibn Ibrahim were with them in and around Mecca, living comfortably without being transgressed by anyone. Later, Rabia'a ibn Haritha ibn Amr ibn Aamer, who was known as Luhi, married Fahirah the daughter of Aamer ibn Amr ibn al-Harith ibn Madhadh ibn Amr al-Jurhumi, the king of Jurhum. She gave birth to a boy named Amr. He was Amr ibn Luhi. He reached a highly prestigious and honorable status in Mecca and among the Arabs that had never been reached before. He was a very wealthy man. He gouged out the eyes of 20 camels, which was a tradition in the pre-Islamic era among Arabs. When a man owned a thousand camels, he gouged out the eyes of one of them (to avoid being envied).

"He was the first to feed the pilgrims who came to visit Mecca and he offered them camel meat and Thareed (a type of thin bread). He also distributed three Yamani cloaks to every pilgrim. His high honor among Arabs was so great that they followed everything he said as if it was a religion to them. He was the first to set rules regarding camels, like Bahar al-Bahirah [بحر البحيرة][92], which involved a female camel that no one could ride nor consume its milk, fur, or meat, except for guests.

"He also established Wasal al-Wasilah [وصل الوصيلة], so that if a female camel gave birth to male camels six times [it could be eaten], but if the seventh birth produced twin camels, one female and the other male, it could not be eaten. Another tradition that he established was Hama al-Hami [حمى الحامي], which meant that if a male camel impregnated female camels ten times, it was to be called Hami and was not to be ridden or used to carry goods. Also, [he established] Saiyab al-Sai'bah [سيب السائبة], [so when a] camel was gifted to the idols, no one could eat it or use its milk.

"Amr ibn Luhi was also the first to bring (the idol) Hubal from Heet in the Arabian peninsula. He set it in the middle of the Ka'ba, where the Quraysh and other Arabs used to cast lots by arrows in front of it. He was the first to change the Hanifiyyah (monotheism), the religion of Ibrahim.

"There was in Mecca a man from Jurhum who did not change his religion [or Hanifiyyah] and he was a poet. He came to Amr ibn Luhi when he changed the religion of Ibrahim and said to him, 'oh Amr, do not do unjust acts in Mecca; it is a sacred place where all the creatures are respected and treated fairly.' It is said that Amr ibn Luhi expelled the Jurhumi man from Mecca and he went to a place near al-Medina.

"The situation in Mecca did not change: Amr ibn Luhi and his offspring ruled Mecca for 500 years. The last one [to rule] was Hulail ibn Habashiya ibn Salul ibn Kaab ibn Amr. He married his daughter Huba bint Hulail to Qusai and they were the rulers of Mecca and servants of the Ka'ba. The House remained in a good state during that time. The Khuza'i did not build any new additions in it after the

---

92. The principle behind Bahar al-Bahirah, the keeping of an animal to feed guests, remains an important part of Bedouin code of desert hospitality to this day.

Jurhum and they did not steal anything from the Ka'ba; they kept glorifying and defending it. Amr ibn al-Harith ibn Amr al-Ghabashani wrote in a poem:
> we ruled the House without cheating,
> but Ibn al-Madhadh was not ruling it fairly;
> he was stealing its treasures,
> but we did not touch or steal anything from it."

124 - Muḥammad ibn Yahya narrated to me, saying, Abdul Aziz ibn Imran narrated to us, saying: "Before Islam, a man called Abu Salama ibn Abdul-Asad al-Makhzumi went towards al-Yaman with a group of men from the Quraysh. On the road they became very thirsty and they lost their way. Abu Salama said to them, 'I want to set my camel free and follow it; what is your say?' They said, 'do that.' He did so and followed it until they reached a place with water. They drank from it and gave drink to their camels. While they were there, a man approached them and asked, 'who are you?' They answered, 'we are from Quraysh.' The man went to a tree and he said something there. Then he came back and said, 'can one of you come with me? There is a man who wants to speak to you.' Abu Salama said, 'I went with him and we stood under the tree. There was a den in it. The man started calling loudly, "father, father!" An old man peeked his head out.' The younger man said to him, 'here is the man.' [The man in the den] asked, 'who are you?' Abu Salama replied, 'I am from Quraysh.' The old man asked, 'from which sub-clan?' He replied, 'from Bani-Makhzum ibn Yaqadhah.' The old man asked, 'which one?' He replied, 'Abu Salama ibn Abdul-Asad ibn Hilal ibn Abdullah ibn Umar ibn Makhzum ibn Yaqadhah.' The old man said, 'oh, Yaqadhah is the same age as me! Do you know who said:
> as if no one has ever resided between al-Safa and al-Juhun,
> and no one has ever dwelled in Mecca.
> We were the people of Mecca
> and we have been exiled by the vicissitudes of time.

Abu Salama responded, 'no, I do not.' The old man said, 'I said it. I am Amr ibn al-Harith ibn Madhadh al-Jurhumi. Do you know why (the area of) Ajyad is called Ajyad?' Abu Salama said, 'no, I do not.' The old man said, 'because it was full of blood during our war with Qedar. Do you know why (the area of) Qaiqa'an is called Qaiqa'an?' Abu Salama said, 'no, I do not.' The man said, 'because of the loud sound of metal weapons on the day we fought Qedar.'"

Chapter Three

The Guardianship of the Ka'ba; The Responsibilities of Al-Siqayah, Al-Rifadah, and Al-Qiyadah

125 - Abu al-Walid narrated to us, saying, my grandfather narrated to me, saying, Sa'id ibn Salim narrated to us, on the authority of Uthman ibn Saj, on the authority of Ibn Jurayj and on the authority of Ibn Ishaq, one of them adding to the other, who said:

"The Khuza'i resided in Mecca and ruled the House for 300 years. A ruler of Tubba' marched toward Mecca in an attempt to ruin the House and destroy it. Khuza'i defended the House and fought strongly until they pushed [the men of Tubba'] back to where they came from. Another ruler from Tubba' repeated the attempt and was also defeated by Khuza'i. The third ruler came during the time of Quraysh. He slaughtered animals for the House, made a covering for the Ka'ba, and made a key for the Ka'ba door. He stayed for several days in the (Forbidden) House; every day he gave orders to slaughter one hundred animals—neither he nor anyone of his army ate from them. [The slaughtered animals] were given to people who lived in the mountain passes and pathways of Mecca. [The people] took what they needed and then left [the rest] to birds of prey to eat from until the night, when predators came to eat what had been left. The king went back to al-Yaman afterward.

"Before that, during the time of the Khuza'i, while the Quraysh was divided among the Bani-Kinanah, a group of pilgrims from Bani-Qudha'a came to Mecca. Among them was man called Rabi'a ibn Haram ibn Dhabbah ibn Abd ibn Kabeer ibn Adhrah ibn Sa'd ibn Zaid. Kilab ibn Murrah ibn Kaab ibn Luai ibn Ghalib had died. He left two sons, Zahra and Qusai, with their mother Fatima bint Amr ibn Saad ibn Sail. Her grandfather Saad ibn Sail was well known for his bravery. It is said that he was the bravest man in his time which inspired some poets to compose whole poems about his courage. When Rabi'a ibn Haram, the pilgrim from Bani-Qudha'a, was in Mecca, he married Fatima (Kilab's widow). Rabi'a took Fatima back with him to the land of Adhrah in al-Sham. Zahra, Fatima's older boy, who was an adult, stayed in Mecca and did not go with his mother. His brother Qusai was a newly weaned child, and his mother took him with her.

"Fatima gave birth to a boy who was named Razah ibn Rabi'a. Razah was Qusai's half-brother on his mother's side. Rabi'a ibn Haram had three other boys from another woman, named Hin, Mahmud, and Jalhamah.

"While Qusai was in the land of Qudha'a, he did not feel that he belonged there, apart from to his stepfather Rabi'a ibn Haram. When Qusai reached the age of puberty, a man from Qudha'a said to him, 'why don't you go back to your people? You are not one of us.' Qusai went back to his mother and asked her about what the man said. She said to him, 'oh son, by the Lord you are better than him and more honorable. You are the son of Kilab ibn Murrah ibn Kaab ibn Luai ibn Ghalib ibn Fihr ibn Malik ibn al-Nadhir bin Kinanah. Your people live by the Forbidden House and in the area around it.'

"Qusai decided to go back to his people because he hated living like an outsider in the land of Qudha'a. His mother said to him, 'oh son, do not be hasty. Wait until the Haram month begins, then you can go with the pilgrims. I fear the road might be dangerous.' Qusai obeyed his mother and waited for the Haram month, then he set off with the pilgrims of Qudha'a. When he reached Mecca, he performed his pilgrimage and settled there.

"Qusai was a strong, tough, and clever man. He proposed to marry Huba bint Hulail, the daughter of Hulail ibn Habashiya ibn Salul al-Khuza'i. When Hulail knew the lineage of Qusai, he happily approved their marriage. At that time Hulail was the guardian of the Ka'ba and the ruler of Mecca.

"Qusai lived with him until [Qusai's] wife gave birth to Abdul-Dar, who was Qusai's older son—then Abdu-Manaf, Abdul-Ezza, and Abd. Hulail was responsible for opening the House, but if he was unwell he gave the key to his daughter, Huba, to open the House. If she was unwell, she gave the key to her husband Qusai or one of her sons to open it.

"Qusai intended to keep the House and rule the people of Khuza'i. When Hulail was dying, he thought about Qusai and his many sons from his daughter. He asked Qusai to come and told him that he decided to give him the honor of guarding the House. He handed him the key which was kept in Huba's house. After the death of Hulail, the Khuza'i did not want Qusai to be the guardian of the House and they took the key from Huba. Qusai went to seek the support of his people from the Quraysh and Bani-Kinanah and asked for their backing. They agreed to support him at his request.

"Then Qusai sent to his half-brother Razah ibn Rabi'a who was living with his people of Qudha'a and asked for his backing. [Qusai] told him what Khuza'i did to prevent him his right of guarding the House. Razah spoke to his people, asking for support for his brother, and they agreed to go with him. He set off with his other half-brothers from his father's side: Hin, Mahmud, and Jalhamah, the sons of Rabi'a ibn Haram, along with a group from Bani-Qudha'a and the Arab pilgrims.

"When the people gathered in Mecca they performed Hajj. On the last day of Mina (the last day of the Hajj), the people from Qudha'a sent to the people of Khuza'i asking them to give Qusai his right that was given to him by Hulail. [The people of Qudha'a] reminded them of the sacredness of the House and the great sin of fighting in it. They also warned [the Khuza'i] of committing transgression in Mecca and reminded them of what had happened to Jurhum when they did so. Khuza'i refused to hand the key to Qusai and they battled each other at a place in Mina which was later called al-Mufjir[93] because of the sacrilege and the blood that

---

93. In Arabic, al-Mufjir means "committing great sins."

was shed there. Each side fought brutally and the death toll was high on both sides with many casualties.

"The Arab pilgrims from Madhar and Yaman did not take part in the fight and they intervened to make peace between the two sides. They finally agreed to choose one man from the Arabs to judge between them. They chose a noble man called Ya'mur ibn Aouf ibn Kaab ibn Aamer ibn al-Layth ibn Bakr ibn Abdu-Munat ibn Kinanah. He said to them, 'we are meeting tomorrow at the courtyard of the Ka'ba.'

"People gathered there at the agreed time; they counted the dead men on both sides and the numbers were higher for the Khuza'i than the Quraysh, Qudha'a, and Bani-Kinanah. Not all the tribes of the Bani-Kinanah entered this war to support Qusai—there was only a small number of tribes with the Quraysh. The whole tribe of Bakr ibn Abdu-Munat did not take part. When people gathered at the courtyard of the Ka'ba, Ya'mur ibn Aouf stood up and said, 'I have put the blood that was shed between you under my feet[94] and from now on no one should seek revenge from the other side. I have judged that Qusai is the trustee and guardian of the Ka'ba, and the ruler of Mecca, because Hulail entrusted him to do so. No one should deny him his right. On the other hand, Khuza'i should stay in their houses in Mecca and no one should force them out.' It is said that Yamur was named al-Shaddakh after that day.

"Khuza'i handed the key to Qusai and they regretted shedding blood in the Sanctuary. Qusai was in charge of guarding the Ka'ba and ruling Mecca. He brought the people of the Quraysh to Mecca to support him and give him more power. He did not force Khuza'i out; they stayed in their houses as before, and they are still there to this day.

"Qusai composed a poem to thank his brother Razah ibn Rabi'a, mentioning in it his noble ancestry that goes back to prophet Ismail's sons, and how he dominated Mecca with the help and support of his brother. Qusai was the first man from Bani-Kinanah to become a king and to be obeyed by his people. He was responsible for providing water for pilgrims [siqayah], providing food for the pilgrims [rifadah], keeping the key of the Ka'ba [hijabah]. He also built a house to assemble the noblemen of the Quraysh to discuss the various issues about Mecca and the Ka'ba [al-Nadwa] and oversaw the army [qiyadah] and the flag [liwaa'].

"It is said that the Quraysh were called by this name because of their unity and support for Qusai. Abdulazeez ibn Ismail al-Halabi said, 'the word taqarrush means gathering.' It is said the Qusai was called al-Qurashi, and he was the first to be called by this name. Some others say that al-Nadhir ibn Kinanah was also called al-Qurashi. It is also said that the Quraysh were called by this name because they were trading and dominating that area and earning a great deal of money, therefore people used to say they are like sharks[95] in the sea."

---

94. In Arabic shadakhtu, meaning he has stopped the shedding of blood.
95. In Arabic 'qursh,' قرش.

126 - Abu al-Hasan al-Walid ibn Aban al-Razi narrated to me, on the authority of Ali ibn Ja'far ibn Muḥammad, on the authority of his father, who said:

"it was asked of Ibn Abbas, 'why are the Quraysh named by this name?' He answered, 'because of a sea animal known as Quraysh.' The proof of that is what Tubba' said, 'Quraysh is a sea creature that eats everything and does not leave anything worthy to other animals—just as the tribe of Quraysh dominate everything. A prophet will come from them at the end of time, and blood-shedding will increase amongst them.'

"Then he (Ibn Abbas) referenced what was said by Ibn Jareeh and Muḥammad ibn Ishaq, 'Qusai earned the honor of ruling Mecca and built Dar al-Nadwa, which is a place where the Quraysh gather and decide about various issues. Besides Qusai's sons and their allies, no one from the Quraysh could enter Dar-Alnadwa except if they were 40 years old or older.

"'Abdu-Manaf, who was Qusai's second son, had gained a very prestigious and honorable status during his father's lifetime. [This status] was not achieved by his other brothers nor by any other man of the Quraysh. Abdul-Dar, the older son, was dearly loved by Qusai and his wife Huba. They were concerned about him because of his younger brother's superior status. Huba said to Qusai, "by Allah, I will not be satisfied until you assign something to Abdul-Dar to match his brother's status." Qusai responded, "by Allah, I will make his status equal to his brother's, and I will support him with an honorable position. The people of Quraysh will enter the Ka'ba by his permission only, and they will only gather and discuss their important issues in his presence."

"'Qusai decided to divide the six honorable roles between his two sons. He gave Abdul-Dar the duties of al-Sidanah, Dar al-Nadwa, and al-Liwaa'. He gave Abdu-Manaf the duties of al-Siqayah, al-Rifadah, and al-Qiyadah.

"'Al-Siqayah was performed in Qusai's day by putting leather basins in the courtyard of the Ka'ba and filling them with fresh water. The water was brought by camels from wells so that the pilgrims could drink. Al-Rifadah was a fee paid every year by the people of Quraysh to Qusai so he could prepare food for the pilgrims who could not afford to buy it. When Qusai died, the Quraysh maintained the same traditions that Qusai performed in his time.

"Abdul-Dar was responsible for running Dar al-Nadwa, al-Liwaa', and al-Sidanah. He had command of them until he died. He ordered that his son Uthman ibn Abdul-Dar would take responsibility of al-Sidanah (or Hijabah, as called by some) after him. His other son, Abdul-Manaf ibn Adbul-Dar, took responsibility for running Dar al-Nadwa. The sons of Abdu-Manaf ibn Abdul-Dar continued running Dar al-Nadwa after their father died.

"'If the Quraysh wanted to meet in [Dar al-Nadwa] to discuss issues, the Dar was opened to them by Aamer ibn Hashim ibn Abdu-Manaf ibn Abdul-Dar or by one of his sons or his nephews. Among the traditions that were practiced by the Quraysh in Dar al-Nadwa was that if a slave girl reached the age of puberty the [Quraysh] brought her inside the Dar and one of the sons of Abdu-Manaf ibn Abdul-Dar dressed her in a long, wide dress and sent her back to her family to veil her. Therefore, Aamer ibn Hashim ibn Abdu-Manaf ibn Abdul-Dar was named Maheedh.[96]

"'The sons of Uthman ibn Abdul-Dar continued their responsibilities of al-Hijabah [or al-Sidanah] until after the death of their father. Then [the role] was given to Abdul-Ezza ibn Uthman ibn Abdul-Dar, and then to his son Abu-Talhah Abdullah ibn Abdul-Ezza ibn Uthman ibn Abdul-Dar, and his son after him, until the day of the Conquest of Mecca when the prophet Muḥammad took [the key] from them and opened the Ka'ba and entered it.

"'When the prophet exited the Ka'ba, he was holding the key. Al-Abbas ibn Abdul-Muttalib said to him, "oh messenger of Allah, may my father and mother be sacrificed for you! Give us al-Hijabah and al-Siqayah." Then Allah the Almighty revealed to his prophet this verse, *"God commands you to return trusts to their rightful owners"* (Qur'an 4:58). Umar ibn al-Khattab said, "that was the first time I heard this verse from the prophet."

"'The prophet recited the verse, then he asked for Uthman ibn Talhah and gave him the key and said, "hide it." Then he said, "oh sons of Abi-Talhah, take it under Allah's care and perform righteous deeds in it; it remains yours forever. None can take it from you except an oppressor."

"'When Uthman ibn Talhah migrated with the prophet, his cousin Shaibah ibn Uthman ibn Abi Talhah took the responsibility of al-Hijabah with his son and his nephew Wahb ibn Uthman until the time when Uthman ibn Talhah ibn Abi Tahla came back from al-Medina after spending a long time there. When he came back, he shared the responsibility of Hijabah with his cousins, and it became the responsibility of all the sons of Abi Talhah.

"'Al-Liwaa', on the other hand, was the responsibility of all the sons of Bani Abdul-Dar, taken first by the oldest and the most honorable during the pre-Islamic era until the day of the Battle of Uhud when a number of them were killed while holding it (the banner).

"'Al-Siqayah, al-Rifadah, and al-Qiyadah remained for Abdu-Manaf ibn Qusai who was committed to their maintenance until he died. He ordered that after his death his son Hashim ibn Abdu-Manaf ibn Qusai would take the responsibility of al-Siqayah and al-Rifadah while his other son Abd-Shams ibn Abdu-Manaf was given the responsibility of al-Qiyadah.

"'Hashim ibn Abdu-Manaf was feeding the pilgrims every year by collecting whatever money he received from the Quraysh which he used to buy flour. He took the thigh of every slaughtered cow or sheep which he gathered with the flour and cooked to feed the pilgrims. He continued doing that until the year Mecca was

---

96. From the Arabic word *haidh* which means menstruation.

struck by a drought. That year Hashim ibn Abd-Manaf went to al-Sham with the money he had and bought some flour and a type of dry cake or bread [*ka'k*, كعك]. He returned to Mecca at the time of the Hajj with what he bought. Hashim took the *ka'k* he brought and smashed it, and he slaughtered animals and cooked it all, making *thareed* out of it. He fed people with that food until they became full which was the reason he was called Hashim.[97] His real name was Amr.

"'A poet called Ibn al-Zaba'ari al-Sahmi composed a poem about the Quraysh saying:

Quraysh was an egg
and when it cracked, the whole yolk [or essence]
was the share of Abdu-Manaf;
they are well known for their generosity and hospitality,
and they support the poor
until they become equal to the comfortable.
Amr al-Ula smashed the thareed for the people in Mecca
who were hit by draught.

Amr al-Ula the poet refers to Hashim.

"'Hashim ibn Abdu-Manaf fulfilled his responsibility until he died. After that his son Abdul-Muttalib fulfilled the role until he died and after him his son Abu-Talib did it every year during the Hajj until the time of Islam.

"'In year nine of Islam, the prophet sent money with Abu-Bakr when he went to Hajj with others [in order to] prepare food for them. The same thing was done again when the prophet performed the Farewell Pilgrimage. When Abu-Bakr became the caliph, he continued feeding the pilgrims. The same was done by Umar at the time of his caliphate, and by the other caliphs after him, up until the present time. People in Mecca and Mina have the food of Hajj until the end of the Hajj season.

"'Al-Siqayah was also done by Abdu-Manaf. He brought water from a well known as Karadim because he found the water to be fresh. Then he put it in leather basins in the courtyard of the Ka'ba so the pilgrims could use it until they left Mecca.

"'Qusai dug several wells in Mecca. At that time, the water was scarce there and people were drinking from a well located outside the Haram. The first well that Qusai dug in Mecca was known as al-A'jool [العجول]; it was at the house of Um-Hani, the daughter of Abu-Talib, in a place called al-Hazurah. The Arabs used to drink from that well when they came to Mecca. Qusai dug another well at the upper Radm, at the house of Abban ibn Uthman, which belonged to the family of Jahsh ibn Ri'ab before that. That well collapsed and was dug again by Jubayr ibn Mati'm ibn Odai ibn Nawfal ibn Abdu-Manaf.

---

97. In Arabic, Hashim is a person who smashes things.

"'Another well was Badr which was dug by Hashim ibn Abdu-Manaf. When the well was ready he said, 'I will make it a destination for people.' It was located at the back of al-Talub's house, the servant of Zubaidah, at al-Bathaa in a place called al-Mustanthir. Some of the sons of Hashim used to say, "we dug Badr, near al-Mustanthir, to provide water to the pilgrims." Hashim dug another well called Sajlah which is also named the well of Jubayr ibn Muta'm. Part of it is inside the house of al-Quareer.

"'Sajlah continued to be owned by Hashim ibn Abdu-Manaf, and by his sons after him, until it was gifted by Asad ibn Hashim to Muta'm ibn Odai, after Abdul-Muttalib dug Zamzam and they did not need Sajlah anymore. It is also said that Sajlah was gifted to Muta'm by Abdul-Muttalib after digging Zamzam. Muta'm asked for Abdul-Muttalib's permission to put a leather basin near Zamzam so he could bring water from his well, and he was permitted to do so. Hashim ibn Abdu-Manaf continued providing water for pilgrims until he died. Then his son Abdul-Muttalib ibn Hashim resumed [this responsibility] until he dug Zamzam. The existence of Zamzam ended the need for any other well in Mecca, and all pilgrims drank from it.'"

The narrator continued: "Abdul-Muttalib owned many camels. During the season of pilgrimage, he used to gather all his camels and collect their milk and mix it with honey and put it in a leather basin near Zamzam. He also used to buy raisins to put in Zamzam's water to make it taste less strong. The people of Mecca used to put water skins in their houses to store water, and they sweetened it with handfuls of raisins and dates. Fresh water was very rare in Mecca; it could only be found in the Well of Maimoon or wells outside Mecca. Abdul-Muttalib continued providing water for pilgrims until he died and his son al-Abbas ibn Abdul-Muttalib resumed the responsibility after his father.

"Al-Abbas owned a grape orchard in al-Ta'if; he used to lend money to the people of al-Ta'if and they paid him back with raisins. He put all the raisins in the drinking water for the pilgrims, during the Hajj, during the pre-Islamic time and at the beginning of Islam.

"On the Day of the Conquest, the prophet entered Mecca and seized the Siqayah from al-Abbas ibn Abdul-Muttalib, and the Hijabah from Uthman ibn Talhah. Al-Abbas stood up and stretched his hand and said to the prophet, 'oh messenger of Allah, may my father and mother be sacrificed for you! Give us both al-Hijabah and al-Siqayah.' The prophet said, 'do you want me to give you both privileges?' Then he stood between the two jambs of the door of Ka'ba and said, 'all the customs of pre-Islamic times [or Jahiliyya] of money, blood, and revenge are destroyed except Siqayah and Sidanah [or Hijabah] which I will give back to the people who were responsible for them during the pre-Islamic time.'

"Al-Abbas took the Siqayah again and he served until he died. Then his son Abdullah ibn al-Abbas fulfilled the responsibility of Siqayah rather than his other siblings. Muḥammad ibn al-Hanafiyyah talked to Ibn al-Abbas about the Siqayah (he wanted to do the job), and Ibn al-Abbas said, 'for what reason? We have more right to it than you do both in Jahiliya and in Islam; your father had also addressed it and I clarified the proof of our right, along with Talhah ibn Ubaydellah, Aamer ibn Rabi'a, Azhar ibn Abd ibn Aouf, and Makhramah ibn Nawfal that al-Abbas ibn Abdul-Muttalib succeeded his father Abdul-Muttalib during the time of Jahiliyya while your grandfather was doing other business and taking care of his camels. The prophet gave this responsibility to al-Abbas rather than the rest of the sons of Abdul-Muttalib on the Day of Conquest of Mecca, and all the people who were present on that day knew that. The responsibility of Siqayah went to Abdullah ibn Abbas after his father's death; no one has ever disputed his right to do so until he died. It then moved to his son Ali ibn Abdullah ibn Abbas who was doing the same as his father and grandfather, [buying] raisins and bringing them from al-Ta'if to soak in Zamzam water. He did this until he died and the responsibility of al-Siqayah continued to move from one generation of his offspring to the next up to the present time.

"On the other hand, the responsibility of al-Qiyadah went to Abdu-Shams ibn Abdu-Manaf; after him it passed to Umayah ibn Abdu-Shams, then to Harb ibn Umayah who lead the people in the day of Okadh [عُكاظ][98] in the war between the Quraysh and Qais Ailan, and also in the first and second daily prayer [or Fajr]. Before that, he led the people in Thata Nakeef (ذات نكيف) in the war between the Quraysh and the Bani-Bakr ibn Abdu-Munat ibn Kinanah, when the Ahabeesh were allied with Bani-Bakr. They entered into an alliance with them against the Quraysh on a mountain named al-Habashi, therefore they were named Ahabeesh. After that, Abu-Sufyan ibn Harb led the Quraysh after his father until the Day of Badr,[99] when the people of Quraysh were led by Rabi'a ibn Abdu-Shams because Abu-Sufyan was [away] leading a caravan. Abu-Sufyan again led the Quraysh on the Day of Uhud[100] and on the Day of al-Ahzab[101] which was the last major incident [or significant battle] for the Quraysh and Harb until the Day of the Conquest of Mecca."[102]

---

98. Suq Okadh was a market near the holy city that operated for two weeks every year.
99. The Day of Badr was the first of several important Muslim victories in their war with the Quraysh on 13 March 624 CE (17 Ramadan, 2 AH).
100. A battle where the Muslims defeated the Quraysh on 23 March, 625 CE (7 Sawwal, 3 AH).
101. *Ahzab* means confederates. Its mention here refers to the Battle of the Trench (c. spring 627 CE); these events are detailed in chapter 33, Al-Ahzab, in the Qur'an.
102. Muḥammad seized Mecca from the Quraysh, largely unopposed, in December 629 or January 630 CE (10-20 Ramadan, 8 AH).

> There are interesting correlations between Roman and Muslim history, especially regarding the Muslim Day of Conquest. One common objection to Petra as the original Holy City of Islam is the fact that Petra was part of the Roman empire. Muḥammad captured the Holy City from the Quraysh, not the Romans. However, at the time of the Muslim conquest of the Holy City, the Romans had not been in control of Petra for 17 years due to the sweeping gains of the Sassanians. The Roman loss of Syria and Palestine to the Sassanians coincides exactly with the beginning of Muḥammad's preaching (613 CE), and the conclusive Roman defeat in Jerusalem coincides with the start of the Quraysh's persecution of the Muslims (614 CE). A power vacuum was created in the Roman empire east of the Jordan—one that the Quraysh could fill. The Qur'an also specifically mentions these events, which is remarkable because the Qur'an seldom provides historical context—see Surah 30. Muslim history fits into the history of Roman Petra.
>
> For further information, see chapter 13 of *Let the Stones Speak* entitled "The Roman Army."

Ismail's Progeny Turn to Idol Worship; Amr ibn Luhi Changes the Hanifiyyah

127 – Abu al-Walid narrated to us, saying, my grandfather narrated to me, saying, Sa'd ibn Salim narrated to me, on the authority of Uthman ibn Saj, who said, Ibn Ishaq informed me:

"The sons of Ismail and the people of Jurhum started spreading outside Mecca because it became crowded. They travelled looking for new places to live and work. It is said that the worship of stone started with the sons of Ismail, as they used to bring stones from the Haram with them when they travelled outside Mecca. [They did this] because of their love and glorification of the Haram and Mecca. When they settled in a new place, they used to set the stones they brought with them and perform tawaf around them to imitate the tawaf around the Ka'ba. Then they started selecting the stones that they liked the most, especially the stones of the Haram. As generations passed, they started forgetting their religion and traded the religion of Ibrahim and Ismail with the worship of idols. They returned to practicing the wrong deeds and sins of the nations that came before them. They adopted some rituals from the people of Noah and added some of what stayed with them from the religion of Ibrahim and Ismail. They continued glorifying the House, circumambulated around it, performed pilgrimage and Umrah, stood on 'Arafat and Muzdalifah, and sacrificed animals—[but] they added other things that were not originally religious [or part of the religion of Ibrahim].

"Amr ibn Luhi was the first to change the religion of Ibrahim and Ismail and to erect idols. He was also the first to set rules regarding camels such as Saiyab al-Sai'bah, Bahar al-Bahirah, Wasal al-Wasilah, and Hama al-Hami."

128 - My grandfather narrated to us, saying, Sa'id ibn Salim narrated to us, on the authority of Uthman ibn Saj, who said, Ibn Jurayj informed me, saying, Ikrimah, the freedman of Ibn Abbas, on the authority of Ibn Abbas, said:

"The prophet said, 'I saw Amr ibn Luhi dragging his bowels in Hellfire.' The prophet asked him, 'who is in Hellfire?' [Amr ibn Luhi] replied, 'those nations which are between you and me.' The prophet also said, 'he (Amr) was the first to establish the rules of al-Bahirah, al-Sai'bah, al-Wasilah, and Al-Hami, and the first to erect idols around the Ka'ba, and to change the Hanifiyyah, the religion of Ibrahim.'"

Chapter Four

The Idol Hubal and Casting Lots by Arrows

129 - Abu al-Walid narrated to us, saying, my grandfather Ahmad ibn Muḥammad narrated to me, saying, Sa'id ibn Muḥammad narrated to us, saying, Sa'id ibn Salim al-Qaddah narrated to us, on the authority of Uthman ibn Saj, who said, Muḥammad ibn Ishaq informed me, saying:

"The well that was inside the Ka'ba was located on the right-hand side from the door when entering the Ka'ba. It was three cubits deep. It is said that Ibrahim and Ismail dug it to store the gifts that were given to the Ka'ba. It stayed this way until the time of Amr ibn Luhi. He brought an idol called Hubal from the land of al-Jazeera [or the peninsula].

"Hubal was one of the greatest idols of the Quraysh. Amr erected it on the well inside the Ka'ba and he ordered people to worship it. When a man from the Quraysh returned from travel, the first thing he did after arriving in Mecca and doing the tawaf was visit Hubal. [He would] shave his head in front of it, even before seeing his family.

"On the Day of Uhud, Abu-Sufyan said, 'oh Hubal, be lifted up,' which meant, 'reveal to them your religion.' The prophet said, 'Allah is higher and more majestic.'

"The well that was inside the Ka'ba was named al-Akhsaf [الأخسف] and the Arabs called it al-Akhshaf [الأخشف]."

Muḥammad ibn Ishaq said: "there were seven arrows with Hubal in the Ka'ba. On each arrow there was an order [or lot]. On one arrow 'blood-money' was written. [It was used] when they disagreed who should pay it. They used seven arrows and the one who received the arrow that had 'blood-money' on it was the one who paid it."[103]

"On another arrow 'yes' was written, and on another, 'no.' When [the Quraysh] wanted to do something, they drew from the arrows to determine whether they should do that thing or not, and they obeyed what was indicated by the arrows.

"On the rest of the arrows, 'among you,' 'not among you,' 'mulsaq,' and 'water' were written. When they wanted to dig a well for water, they shot the arrow that had 'water' written on it and they dug a well on the spot where the arrow landed. They also used [the arrows] when they wanted to circumcise a boy, get married, bury a dead person, or when they doubted someone's lineage. [When they doubted someone's lineage, the Quryash] brought the person in question to Hubal with one hundred dirhams and an animal to sacrifice. They gave [the money and sacrifice] to the custodian of the arrows and brought the person close to Hubal and said, 'oh our lord, this is so-and-so, and we want to do such-and-such with him or

---

103. Ibn Ishaq explained in *The Life of Muhammad* that the arrows were drawn like lots from a quiver. Ibn Ishaq, *The Life of Muhammad: A Translation of Ibn Ishaq's Sirat Rasul Allah*, trans. A. Guillaume (New York: Oxford University Press), 84.

her. Show us what to do.' Then they said to the custodian, 'draw the lot.' If they drew 'among you,' it meant the person was one of them. If they drew 'not among you,' it meant the person was not one of them. If they drew 'mulsaq,' it meant the person remained in the same condition with no known lineage.

"Regarding the other issues, if they drew 'yes,' they performed the matter in question immediately. If they drew 'no,' they postponed [the matter] one year and then drew the lot again to decide on the matter.

"Abdul-Muttalib used the arrows to decide on slaughtering his son."

Muhammad ibn Ishaq said: "Hubal was made of agate beads in the shape of a human. His right hand was broken off, and the Quraysh repaired it by making a gold hand for [the idol]. Hubal had a vault for tribute. It had seven casting arrows used to decide on issues like dead people, virginity, and marriage. Its offering was one hundred camels and it had a custodian."

Isaf and Nai'la Turned to Stone; The Destruction of the Idols of the Quraysh

130 - Abu al-Walid narrated to us, saying, my grandfather narrated to me, on the authority of Sa'id ibn Salim, on the authority of Uthman ibn Saj, who said, Muhammad ibn Ishaq narrated to me:

"When Jurhum transgressed in the Haram, a man entered the House with a woman and committed an act of obscenity with her. It is also said that he kissed her. Then Allah the Almighty caused them to change into two rocks. The man was called Isaf ibn Bagha' and the woman was called Nai'la bint Dhi'b. After that, they were brought out of the Ka'ba and were erected on the Safa and Marwa [mountains] so the people could be admonished when they saw them and warned not to do the same act. It continued like that until, with time, some people started worshipping them and they became idols. At the time of Amr ibn Luhi, he ordered people to worship and glorify them and he said to the people, 'those who were before you worshipped them.'

"At the time of Qusai ibn Kilab, when he became the governor of Mecca and the servant of the Ka'ba, he removed [Isaf and Nai'la] from al-Safa and al-Marwa and placed one of them close to the Ka'ba's wall and the other near Zamzam. It is said in a different narration that he placed them both near Zamzam. He slew sacrifices in front of them and the people of Jahiliyya touched them when they passed near them. When they performed tawaf, the people started by touching Isaf and ended by touching Nai'la. They continued this until the Day of the Conquest of Mecca when the prophet broke them with the rest of idols."

131 - Muhammad ibn Yahya al-Madani narrated to me, on the authority of Ibrahim ibn Muhammad ibn Abi Yahya, on the authority of Ibn Hazm, on the authority of Amrah, who said:

"Isaf and Nai'la were a man and a woman and they were changed into two rocks. They were taken out of the Ka'ba with their clothes on. One of them was placed close to the Ka'ba and the other near Zamzam. People placed their gifts to the Ka'ba between these two idols. It is said that this place was called al-Hateem. [The rocks] were placed there so people might learn a lesson when they saw them. Things remained that way until they became idols worshipped by people. Whenever the clothes of those idols wore [out], they were replaced. Later, the one that was near the Ka'ba was moved next to the other one near Zamzam and people used to slaughter their sacrifices in front of them. Menstruating women did not come close to them."

132 - My grandfather narrated to me, saying, Sa'id ibn Salim narrated to us, on the authority of Uthman ibn Saj, who said, Ibn Ishaq informed me, on the authority of Abdullah ibn Abi Bakr, on the authority of Ali ibn Abdullah Abbas, who said:

"The prophet entered Mecca on the Day of Conquest and there were 360 idols in it; these idols had been pinned [up] with lead by Iblis [or Satan]. The prophet held a stick and stood in front of the idols and said, *'truth has come, and falsehood perished. Truly, falsehood is ever bound to perish,'* then he pointed at the idols with his stick and they fell off on their backs."

133 - My grandfather narrated to me, on the authority of Sufyan ibn Uyaynah, on the authority of Ibn Abi Najih, on the authority of Mujahid, on the authority of Abu Ma'mar, on the authority of Abdullah ibn Mas'ud:

"There were 360 idols when the prophet entered Mecca on the Day of Conquest. He struck them (with a stick) and said, *'truth has come, and falsehood perished. Truly, falsehood is ever bound to perish. Truth has come and falsehood cannot create anything.'*"

134 - Muḥammad ibn Yahya narrated to us, saying, Abdul Aziz ibn Imran narrated to us, on the authority of Muḥammad ibn Abdul Aziz, on the authority of Ibn Shihab, on the authority of Ubayd Allah ibn Abdullah ibn Utbah ibn Mas'ud, on the authority of Ibn Abbas, who said:

"The prophet entered Mecca and there was 360 idols around the Ka'ba, some of them pinned [up] with lead. The prophet [performed tawaf] on the back of his camel while saying, *'truth has come, and falsehood perished. Truly, falsehood is ever bound to perish.'* He pointed at the idols (with his stick). Whenever the prophet pointed at the face of an idol it fell off on its back, and when he pointed at the back of an idol it fell off face down, until they were all demolished."

Ibn Ishaq said: "after praying the noon prayer on the Day of Conquest, the prophet gave his orders to collect the idols that were around the Ka'ba and burn and break them."

Regarding this Day, Fudhalah ibn Umair ibn al-Mullawah al-Laythi said:

> *"Haven't you seen Muḥammad and his soldiers*
> *on the day of Conquest, when the idols were broken?*
> *You will see the light of Allah become vibrant,*
> *and the disbelief vanish to darkness."*

135 - My grandfather narrated to me, on the authority of Muḥammad ibn Idris, on the authority of al-Waqidi, on the authority of Ibn Abi Sabrah, on the authority of Husayn ibn Abdullah ibn Ubayd Allah ibn Abbas, on the authority of Ikrimah, on the authority of Ibn Abbas, who said:

"The prophet was only pointing at the idol with his stick and that was enough to make it fall off, face down. Then he circumambulated seven times around the Ka'ba on the back of his camel, while touching the Corner with his stick. When the prophet finished the tawaf he dismounted his camel and went to the Maqam. Mua'mar ibn Abdullah ibn Fadhlah came to him and escorted his camel outside the Haram. The prophet was still wearing his armor and his helmet on his head, and his turban [shamlah] was between his shoulders.

"He prayed two Raka'at, then he went to Zamzam and looked down at it and said, 'oh Banu Abdul-Muttalib. Were it not that the people would overwhelm you, I would have drawn water with you.' So al-Abbas ibn Abdul-Muttalib drew up a bucket of water for him and he drank from it. Then the prophet gave his order to demolish Hubal while he was standing in front of it.

"Then al-Zubayr ibn al-Awam said to Abu-Sufyan ibn Harb, 'oh Abu-Sufyan, Hubal has been broken and you were arrogantly claiming on the Day of Uhud that it had done you a favor.' Abu-Sufyan responded, 'desist from saying so. If there was another god [besides] the god of Muḥammad, we would not have met this fate!'"

136 - My grandfather narrated to me, on the authority of Muḥammad ibn Idris, on the authority of al-Waqidi, on the authority of his teachers, who said:

"Isaf and Nai'la were a man and a woman. The man was Isaf ibn Amr, and the woman was Nai'la bint Suhail from Jurhum. They committed adultery inside the Ka'ba and they were transformed into rocks and later worshiped. People sacrificed animals to them and [the people] shaved their heads in front of them during the rituals. When these two idols were broken with the rest of the idols in Mecca, a black [or grey] haired woman got out from one of them. She was scratching her face, naked, and her hair flowed out. [She was] calling for Woe.[104]

"When the prophet was told about her, he said, 'that is Nai'la. She lost all hope to be worshiped in your country ever [again]. It is said that Iblis has cried in pain three times: one time when he was cursed and his appearance changed and became different from the appearance of angels, a second time when he saw the prophet praying in a standing position in Mecca, and a third time when the prophet conquered Mecca. Then Iblis gathered his offspring and said to them, "give up all hope to build disbelief among the people of Muḥammad again after this day and forever. But spread (the custom of) wailing and poetry among them."'"

---

104. It appears the woman is calling for judgment on those who destroyed her idol.

137 - Al-Waqidi mentioned, on the authority of his teachers, who said:

"On the Day of the Conquest of Mecca, the herald of the messenger of Allah made an announcement that 'he who believes in Allah and His messenger, let him break all the idols in his house.' The Muslims started breaking all the idols."

The narrator continued: "when Ikrimah ibn Abi Jahl became a Muslim, he did not leave any idol in any of the houses of the Quraysh. Before Islam he was a trader, making idols and selling them. And all the men of the Quraysh had idols in their houses at that time in Mecca."

138 - Al-Waqidi said, Ibn Abi Sabrah narrated to me, on the authority of Sulayman ibn Suhaym, on the authority of some of the family of Jubayr ibn Mut'im, on the authority of Jubayr ibn Mut'im, who said:

"On the Day of the Conquest of Mecca, the herald of the messenger of Allah made an announcement that 'he who believes in Allah and the Last Day, let him break and burn any idols in his house, and its price is haram.'"

Jubayr said: "before that I saw the idols carried all around Mecca; the Bedouins bought them and carried them back to their houses. All the people of the Quraysh had idols in their houses. They rubbed them, asking for blessing whenever they entered or left their homes."

139 - Al-Waqidi said, Abdul Rahman ibn Abi al-Zinad informed us, on the authority of Abdul Hamid ibn Suhayl, who said:

"When Hind bint Utbah embraced Islam, she broke an idol in her house with a hammer into small pieces while saying, 'we were deceived by you.'"

Chapter Five

Amr ibn Luhi's Idols
140 - Abu al-Walid narrated to us, saying, my grandfather narrated to me, saying, Sa'id ibn Salim al-Qaddah narrated to us, on the authority of Uthman ibn Saj, who said, Ibn Ishaq informed me, saying:

"Amr ibn Luhi erected an idol called Al-Khalsa [الخلصة] at the bottom of Mecca and they hung necklaces on it and gave it wheat and barley as gifts. They also poured milk on it, sacrificed animals to it, and hung ostrich eggs on it. On the mountain of al-Safa he erected an idol called Naheek Mujawid al-Reeh [نهيك مجاود الريح], and on al-Marwa another idol called Muti'm al-Tair [مطعم الطير]."

The Idol Munat
141 - Abu al-Walid narrated to us, saying, my grandfather narrated to me, saying, Sa'id ibn Salim narrated to us, on the authority of Uthman ibn Saj, who said, Muḥammad ibn Ishaq informed me:

"Amr ibn Luhi erected Munat at the seaside near Kadida and it (Munat) belonged to the Azd and Ghassan. They used to glorify it and go on pilgrimage to it. When they circumambulated the House, proceeded from 'Arafat, and finished their visit to Mina, they used to shave their heads in front of Munat. They entered the state of Ihram at Munat, and therefore they did not perform Sa'i between al-Safa and al-Marwa because of the two idols that were on the two mountains— Naheek Mujawid al-Reeh and Muti'm al-Tair. Also, when they started their Ihram to do Hajj or Umrah, they did not allow themselves to be shaded inside a house until they finished their Hajj or Umrah. When a man started his Ihram he did not enter his house, and if he needed something from inside, he would climb from the back of the house.

"After Islam, when the customs of Jahiliyya perished, Allah the Almighty revealed the verse, *'it is not piety that you should come to houses from their rear, but piety is he who is reverent'* (Qur'an 2:189).

The narrator continued: "Munat was worshiped by the Aous, the Khazraj, the Ghassan from the Azd, those who followed their religion from the people of Yathrib, and the people of al-Sham. It was at the seaside, on the side of al-Mushalil in Kadid."

142 - My grandfather narrated to me, on the authority of Sa'id ibn Salim, on the authority of Uthman ibn Saj, who said:

"Munat was for (the tribe of) Hudhail, and it was in Kadid."

Chapter Six

The Idols al-Lat and al-Uzzah

143 - Abu al-Walid narrated to us, saying, my grandfather narrated to me, on the authority of Sa'id ibn Salim, on the authority of Uthman ibn Saj, on the authority of Muḥammad ibn al-Sa'ib al-Kalbi, on the authority of Abu Salih, on the authority of Ibn Abbas:

"There was a man who used to sit on a rock at Thaqeef to sell ghee to the passing pilgrims, and he was kneading [يلت] Saweeq for them. For that reason, people named the rock that he was sitting al-Lat [اللات]. When the man died, people missed him; then Amr told them, 'your God was al-Lat, then he entered the rock.'

"Al-Uzzah was three trees at Nakhlah and the first to call people to worship them was Amr ibn Rabi'a and al-Harith ibn Kaab. Amr told them, 'your god spends the summer in al-Lat because of the cool weather of al-Ta'if and spends the winter in al-Uzzah because of the hot weather of Tahama.' In each of the three trees there was a devil worshiped by the people.

"After the Conquest of Mecca, the prophet sent Khalid ibn al-Walid to cut down al-Uzzah. He did as he was ordered and then he returned to the prophet. The prophet asked him, 'what did you see in them?' Khalid responded, 'nothing.' The prophet said, 'you did not cut them properly. Go back and cut them off.' Khalid went there and cut down what had been left.

"Under the foundation he found a woman with flowing hair looking at what he had cut down as though she was mourning. Khalid came back and said, 'I found such-and-such.' The prophet said, 'I believe you.'"

144 - My grandfather narrated to me, saying, Sa'id ibn Salim narrated to us, on the authority of Uthman ibn Saj, who said, Muḥammad ibn Ishaq informed us:

"Amr ibn Luhi established al-Uzzah in Nakhlah. At the end of the Hajj season, when people finished their tawaf around the Ka'ba, they did not take their Ihram off until they visited Al-Uzzah. They used to circumambulate around it and take their Iharm off there and spend a day near it. It belonged to Khuza'i. The Quraysh and Bani-Kinanah all glorified al-Uzzah as Khuza'i and Madhar did. The custodians who used to serve it were Banu-Shaiban from Bani-Saleem who were allies of the Bani-Hashim."

145 - Uthman said, Muḥammad ibn al-Sa'ib al-Kalbi informed us, saying:

"Banu-Nasr, Jasham, and Saad ibn Bakr, who are branches of the Hawazin tribe, all worshipped al-Uzzah."

Al-Kalbi said: "in each one of al-Lat, al-Uzzah, and Munat, there was a devil which appeared and spoke to the custodians who served them; that is the work of Iblis."

146 - My grandfather narrated to me, on the authority of Muḥammad ibn Idris, on the authority of al-Waqidi, on the authority of Abdullah ibn Yazid, on the authority of Sa'id ibn Amr al-Hudhali, who said:

"The prophet came to Mecca on a Friday, during the last ten days of the month of Ramadan. He sent detachments [sariyah] in every direction and ordered them to raid those who did not embrace Islam. Hisham ibn al-Aasi went out with 200 men to the area of Yalamlam, Khalid ibn Sa'id ibn al-Aasi went out with 300 men to the area of A'rnah, and he sent Khalid ibn al-Walid to demolish al-Uzzah.

"Khalid went out with 30 horsemen [from amongst] his friends to al-Uzzah, and he cut it off. When he came back, the prophet asked him, 'have you cut it down?' He said, 'yes, messenger of Allah.' The prophet said, 'have you seen anything?' Khalid said, 'no.' the prophet said, 'you did not cut it off. Go back and cut it.'

"Khalid ibn al-Walid was angry and went there for the second time. When he arrived, he drew his sword out. Then a black naked women with disheveled hair appeared to him. Her custodians started screaming. Khalid reported, 'I felt shivers at my back.' The custodians cried loudly to al-Uzzah, 'oh Uzzah, launch a severe and matchless attack on Khalid! Oh Uzzah, uncover your mask and demonstrate your power!"

"Khalid approached, raising his sword, and said, 'oh disbeliever, Allah has humiliated you.' Then killed her and went back to the prophet and told him what happened. The prophet said, 'that was al-Uzzah. She gave up hope to be worshiped in this land any longer.'

"After that Khalid said, 'oh messenger of Allah, praise be to Allah who honored us with you, and saved us from destruction by you. I used to see my father approach al-Uzzah and sacrifice the best of his camels and sheep to it. He spent three days at its side until he came back to us in a state of satisfaction and happiness. Now I reflect on how my father had died and how he was pursuing his life. He was misled until he sacrificed (his animals) to a thing that does not hear nor see and does not harm nor benefit.' The prophet said, 'this matter belongs to Allah. For whomever He makes smooth the path of guidance, he will be guided. And whomever He makes smooth the path of misguidance, he will be misguided.' It was demolished in the last five days of Ramadan, year eight.

"The custodian of al-Uzzah was Aflah ibn al-Nadhir al-Salami from Bani-Saleem. When his death approached, Abu-Lahab came to visit him and he found him very sad. Abu-Lahab asked, 'why do you look sad?' He replied, 'I am afraid that al-Uzzah will be neglected after my death.' Abu-Lahab said to him, 'do not be sad; I shall attend to her after you go.' After that, Abu-Lahab told whoever he met, 'if al-Uzzah triumphs, I have already earned a favor for serving her. And if Muḥammad triumphs over al-Uzzah, which I do not believe will happen, he is my nephew.'

After that, Allah the Almighty revealed the verse, *'may the hands of Abu Lahab perish, and may he perish!'*" (Qur'an 111:1).

147 - My grandfather narrated to me, saying, Sufyan ibn Uyaynah narrated to us, on the authority of Abdul Malik ibn Umayr, on the authority of someone who narrated to him, who said:

"Hassan ibn Thabit al-Ansari came to the prophet while he was in the mosque and said, 'oh messenger of Allah, would you grant me your permission to recite (a poem), for I would say nothing but the truth.' The prophet said, 'say it.' Hassan started reciting, 'I witness in the name of Allah that Muḥammad is the messenger of the One who is above the heavens.' The prophet said, 'I testify.' Hassan ibn Thabit resumed, 'and that both Yahya and the father of Yahya have performed deeds that are accepted (by Allah).' The prophet said, 'I testify.' Hassan ibn Thabit said, 'and the Son of Maryam who opposed the Jews was a messenger sent from the Lord of the Throne.' The prophet said, 'I testify.' Hassan said, 'and the brother of al-Ahqaf, who was (continuously) accused (by his people), had fought in the cause of Allah.' The prophet said, 'I testify.' Hassan continued, 'and whoever believes in what was in the tree that is in Batn-Nakhlah goes astray.' The prophet said, 'I testify.'

Sufyan said: "he refered to al-Uzzah because Munat is located in al-Mushalil in Kadid."

The Idol of Dhat-Anwat

148 – Abu al-Walid narrated to us, saying, my grandfather narrated to me, on the authority of Muḥammad ibn Idris, on the authority of Muḥammad ibn Umar al-Waqidi, on the authority of Ma'mar ibn Rashid al-Basri, on the authority of al-Zuhri, on the authority of Sinan ibn Abi Sinan al-Daylami, on the authority of Abu Waqid al-Laythi, who is al-Harith ibn Malik, who said:

"We went out with the prophet to Hunain. There was a great green tree named Dhat-Anwat [ذات أنواط] that belonged to the disbelievers from the Quraysh and other Arab tribes. They visited it every year for an entire day and hung their weapons upon it and sacrificed animals to it."

The narrator continued: "one day, when we were walking with the prophet, we saw a big tree at the side of the road. We said to the prophet, 'oh messenger of Allah, make a Dhat-Anwat for us as they have a Dhat-Anwat.' The prophet responded, 'Allahu-Akhbar, Allahu-Akhbar. By the One in Whose Hand Muḥammad's soul is, this is like what Musa's people said, *"make for us a god as they have gods." He said, "truly you are an ignorant people"'* (Qur'an 7:138). 'These are the traditions [or sunnas] of those who were before you.'"

149 - My grandfather narrated to me, on the authority of Muḥammad ibn Idris, on the authority of al-Waqidi, who said, Ibn Abi Habibah narrated to me, on the authority of Dawud ibn al-Husayn, on the authority of Ikrimah, on the authority of Ibn Abbas, who said:

"Dhat-Anwat was a tree exalted by people of Jahiliyya who spent a day with it and sacrificed to it. When they went to Hajj they left their provisions near it and entered [the Sacred area] without any [provisions], to glorify it. When the prophet was going to Hunain with a group of his companions—one of them was al-Harith ibn Malik—they said, 'oh messenger of Allah, make a Dhat-Anwat for us as they have a Dhat-Anwat.' The prophet uttered takbir and said, 'this is what the people of Musa did to Musa.'"

A similar sacred tree exists today in Jordan, located: 32.066079° 37.147924°. It is primarily visited by Muslims from Asia.

Muḥammad Sends Troops to Demolish the Idols

150 - Abu al-Walid narrated to us, saying, my grandfather narrated to me, on the authority of Muḥammad ibn Idris, on the authority of Muḥammad ibn Umar al-Waqidi, who said, Abdullah ibn Yazid informed me, on the authority of Sa'id ibn Amr al-Hudhali, who said:

"When the prophet conquered Mecca, he sent out troops. Khalid ibn al-Walid was sent to demolish al-Uzzah. Al-Tofail ibn Amr al-Dousi was sent to Dho-Alkafain [ذو الكفين] which was the idol of Amr ibn Hamhamah. Al-Tofail burned the idol while reciting, 'oh you who belong to Kafain, you are not from our war of worship; our origin[105] is older than your origin. I have set flames inside your core.' Also, Sa'id ibn Ubayd al-Ash-hali was sent to al-Mushalil to demolish Munat.

"Amr ibn al-A's was sent to demolish Siwa' [سواع], the idol of (the tribe of) Hudhail. Amr said, 'when we arrived at Siwa', its custodian was there. He said, "what do you want?" I said, "I want to demolish Siwa'." He said, "why would you do that?" I said, "The messenger of Allah ordered me to do so." He said, "you can't demolish it." I asked, "why not?" He said, "he declines." I said, "you still believe the falsehood! Woe to you; can it hear or see anything?" Then I approached the

---
105. "Origin" meaning birth.

idol and broke it, and I ordered my companions to demolish its vault, and there was nothing in it. Then I said to the custodian, "what say you?" He said, "I have submitted to Allah the exalted.""

Tubba's Journey to the Ka'ba

151 - Abu al-Walid narrated to us, saying, my grandfather narrated to me, on the authority of Sa'id ibn Salim, on the authority of Uthman ibn Saj, who said, Ibn Ishaq informed me, saying: "Tubba' al-Awal [تُبَّع الأول], or the first Tubba', marched toward the Ka'ba to ruin and demolish it. Khuza'i ruled Mecca at that time and served at the Ka'ba, so they defended the Ka'ba and resisted Tubba' until he retreated to where he came from. After that, another Tubba' did the same. The Tubba's who wanted to demolish the Ka'ba were three. Before that, some of them visited the Ka'ba and glorified the House whenever they passed near Mecca in their travels. The third Tubba', who wanted to demolish the House, [attempted to demolish it during] the time of the Quraysh."

The narrator continued: "the reason for his attack was because a group from the tribe of Hudhail from Bani-Lahyan came to him and said, 'there is a House in Mecca that is glorified by all the Arabs. They visit it, sacrifice animals to it, and perform Hajj and Umrah in it. It is kept and served by the Quraysh; they have earned its honor, and you are the one who should have this honor. So, if you go to that House and demolish it, and you build your own house, then the Arab pilgrims will come to it instead.'"

The narrator said: "Tubba' made his decision to go to the House."

152 - My grandfather narrated to me, saying, Sufyan ibn Uyaynah narrated to us, on the authority of Musa ibn Isa al-Madani, who said:
"When Tubba' and his army arrived at al-Duf, an area between Amj and A'sfan, their animals halted, and the sky grew dark. Tubba' called the Rabbis [or Akhbar] who were with him and asked them [about these things.] They asked, 'are you planning to do something to the House?' He said, 'I wanted to demolish it.' They said, 'it is better for you to cover it (with a cloth) and slaughter animals for it.' When he did as he was told, the sky cleared again."

In another narration, Ibn Ishaq said: "when Tubba' arrived at al-Duf, a strong wind started blowing and the sky became dark. Tubba' called Rabbis, from the people of the Book, and asked them [about it]. They said, 'are you intending to harm this House?' He told them what the people of Hudhail told him and what he was planning to do to the House. The Rabbis said, 'by Allah, they only want your destruction and the destruction of your people. This is the Forbidden House of Allah; anyone who intends to harm it is destroyed.' Tubba' said, 'what should I do?' They said, 'you should have good intentions toward the House by glorifying it and covering it and treating its people kindly.' Tubba' did as advised; then the sky cleared and the strong wind stopped, and their animals started moving easily.

After that Tubba' ordered the people of Hudhail to be killed and fastened them to crosses because they only came to Tubba' and convinced him to demolish the Ka'ba because they were envious of the Quraysh's status in Mecca.

"Tubba' then continued to Mecca. Their weapons were kept in Qaiqa'an, and it is said that is why the place was called Qaiqa'an. Their horses were kept in Ajyad, and it is said that place was called Ajyad, because of Tubba's horses. Their cooking place was in a mountain pass that was known as the pass of Abdullah ibn Aamir ibn Kareez, and for that reason it was then named al-Matabikh.[106]

"Tubba' spent several days in Mecca. Every day he slaughtered one hundred animals; neither he, nor anyone of his army, ate from them. The meat was given to the people (of Mecca) to eat. [What was left was] left to the birds, and at night predators come to eat what had been left. He did that every day while he was in Mecca. Then he fully covered the Ka'ba with al-O'sb [العُصب] (a Yamani type of fabric) and made a door with a Persian latch on it."

Ibn Jareeh said: "Tubba' was the first to fully cover the Ka'ba. He saw in a dream that he covered the Ka'ba, so he covered it with leather sheets. Then he saw another dream and covered it with al-wasai'l [الوصائل] which was a fabric from al-Yaman. He made a door that could be closed—it was not closed before that.

"Tubba' recited a poem describing his journey:
We covered the House that Allah made sacred,
with good types of fabric.
We spent ten days with it and made a latch for its door.
Then we went back, our flag raised high."

The Habasha Attack al-Yaman

153 - Abu al-Walid narrated to us, saying, my grandfather narrated to me, saying, Sa'id ibn Salim, on the authority of Uthman ibn Saj, on the authority of Muḥammad ibn Ishaq, said:

"A king from Himyar named Zur'a Dhu-Nuwas converted to Judaism, and the people of Himyar followed him. The only ones who did not convert were the people of Najran, who were remnants of the Saba' and were Christians. They were still following the original teachings of the Gospel and some of the disciples' [الحواريين] religion. Their leader was called Abdullah ibn Thamir. Dhu-Nuwas invited them to follow Judaism, but they refused. He gave them the choice (to follow him or be killed) and they chose to be killed. He dug a trench for them and killed them in different ways. Some of them were killed in confinement, and some were thrown into the fire in the trench, except for a [particular] man from Saba'. His name was Daws ibn Dhi-Tha'laban and he fled on a horse until he escaped.

"He went to Caesar and pleaded for his help. Caesar said, 'your country is far away from us, but I will send you to the king of Habasha. He is following our religion and will help you.' When Daws reached the Najashi (the king of Habasha),

---
106. Al-Matabikh means "the cooking place" in Arabic.

he supported him and sent a man called Aryat with him. [The King] said to them, 'if you enter al-Yaman, kill a third of its men and destroy third of its land.' After they reached al-Yaman, a brief battle started and Aryat appeared. Zur'a Dhu-Nuwas came out riding his horse and he entered the sea until he disappeared there and that was his end. Aryat entered al-Yaman and he did as al-Najashi had ordered him.

Abraha and the Elephant
154 - Abu al-Walid narrated to us, saying, my grandfather narrated to me, saying, Sa'id ibn Salim, on the authority of Uthman ibn Saj, on the authority of Muḥammad ibn Ishaq, said:

"When the Habasha conquered the land of Yaman it was ruled by Aryat and Abraha. The status of Aryat was superior to that of Abraha, and [Aryat] settled in Yaman for two years, with no one disputing his authority. After that, Abraha decided to strip Aryat of his authority and become the king. There were many troops from al-Habasha and they divided; each half joined one side. The two sides marched towards one another. Aryat was in Sana'a and its surrounding area, while Abraha was in al-Jund and its surrounding area. When the two sides approached each other, Abraha sent to Aryat saying, 'you will destroy (the troops of) al-Habasha between us, so come out against me and let us fight each other and whoever strikes his opponent will have the troops of the other to join him.' Aryat sent to him saying, 'that is a just proposal.' Aryat marched out against Abraha. He was a powerful, tall, and handsome man, and held a spear in his hand. Abraha, on the other hand, was a short fleshy and stocky man with a strong Christian faith. Behind Abraha was a slave boy protecting his back; his name was Atudah.

"When the two opponents drew close to each other, Aryat held his spear high and struck Abraha with it, aiming at the front of Abraha's head, but the spear ripped his eyebrow, eye, nose, and lips; for that reason, Abraha was called al-Ashram.[107] After that, Atudah, Abraha's slave, attacked Aryat with a spear from behind Abraha and killed him. Accordingly, the troops that were with Aryat joined Abraha's troops, and all the (people of) Habasha in Yaman joined his side as well. Everything that Abraha did was without the knowledge of al-Najashi, the king of Habasha in the land of Aksum.

"When the news reached al-Najashi, he became furious and said, 'he attacked my commander and killed him without my approval!?' He then took an oath not to leave Abraha until he conquered his land and cut off his forelock. When Abraha heard about that, he shaved his head and filled a sack with the soil of Yaman and sent it to al-Najashi and wrote to him saying, 'oh king, Aryat was your slave, and I am your slave; we disagreed on your orders but we are all obedient to you. -However, I was more capable of ruling al-Habasha than he was, and more righteous and upright to the people of Yaman than him. I shaved all my head when I heard about the king's oath, and I sent it to him with a sack full of the soil of my land to put it under his feet, and by that, he shall fulfill his oath.' When Al-Najashi received this,

107. Al-Ashram means "harelipped" in Arabic.

he became content with Abraha, and wrote to him, 'stay in the land of Yaman until you hear from me.'

"Abraha settled in al-Yaman and built al-Qalis [القليس], a cathedral at Sana'a. He perfected its construction and named it al-Qalis. Then he sent a message to Al-Najashi saying, 'I have built a church for you. Nothing like it has ever been built for any other king before. I shall not stop until I divert all the Arab pilgrims to it.'"

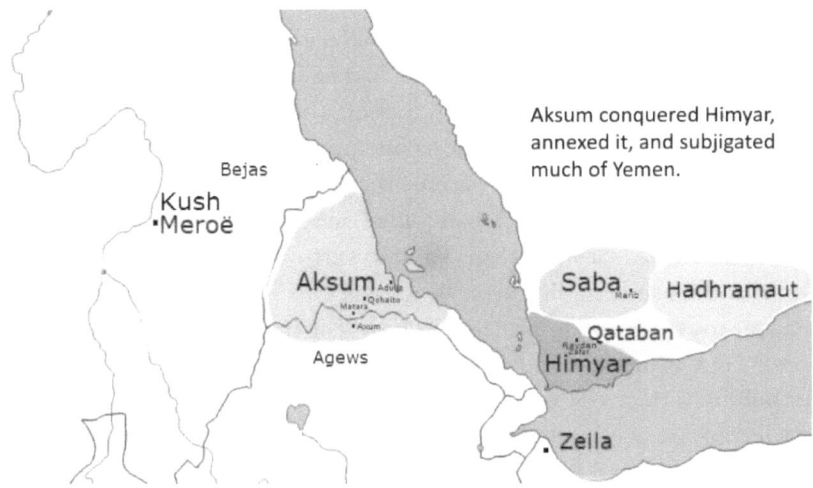

155 - Abu al-Walid said, Muḥammad ibn Yahya informed me, saying:
"I have been told by trusty sheikhs from the people of Yaman at Sana'a that when Allah the Almighty drowned Yousuf Dhu-Nuwas (the one who dug-out the trench in which he burned the people of the book at Najran), al-Habasha came to the land of Yaman through Dahluk[108] until they entered Sana'a. They burned down Ghamdan, which was the greatest castle on earth, and they conquered al-Yaman. Then Abraha al-Habashi built al-Qalis and wrote to al-Najashi saying, 'I have built a house for you. Neither the Arabs nor the Ajam [or non-Arabs] have ever built anything similar to it, and I shall not stop until I divert the Arab pilgrims to it and make them abandon their House.'

"He built al-Qalis using stones from the palace of Balqees at Ma'rib. Balqees was the owner of the building that is mentioned in the Qur'an in the story of (prophet) Sulyman. When Sulyman married Balqees, he visited her at that palace. The builders arranged themselves to transport the stones and the machinery until they carried all the stones, marble, and tools that they needed, and they worked very hard to build it.

"The building (or al-Qalis) was square with equal sides. It was 60 cubits tall in the sky and its internal structure was ten cubits tall. Marble stairs were fitted to climb its entrance, and it was surrounded from all sides by a wall that was 200

---
108. Dahluk is directly west of Sana'a, across the Red Sea: 15.61335 40.0965.

cubits away from al-Qalis. All of it was built by using a type of stone that the people of Yaman call al-Groop [الجـروب]. They were engraved matching stones that were pressed firmly together to the extent that even a needle could not be pressed against it. The length of the wall that was built using the Groop stones was 20 cubits tall. The Groop stones were separated by using other triangular stones, which were interlaced together in a pattern: a green stone, a red stone, a white stone, a yellow stone, and a black stone. Between each of the two rows of these stones they fitted (logs of) Sasim wood which had a rounded front. The logs were thick enough to fit into a grown man's lap and were sticking out of the wall. The building was constructed using this feature.

Al-Qalis was constructed with a common Abyssinian (Habasha) method. It involved interchanging layers of stone and wooden logs. Pictured above is the Debre-Dammo monastery in Tigrinya. Notice how the logs protrude—Azraqi writes that the logs of al-Qalis were large enough to fit into a grown man's lap.

b. Debra Damo. Porch (original west front on right) (From Buxton)

Aobve: a photo of Debre-Dammo taken by K.A.C. Creswell, published in 1951.[109]

"Then there was a decorative marble molding that was two cubits high; it was sticking out from the rest of the wall by one cubit. Above the marble molding, there were sparkling black stones brought from Naqm, the mountain of Sana'a, and above that they put yellow sparkling stones, and then white sparkling stones on top. This was the external look of the walls of al-Qalis. The width of the wall was six cubits. (The Yamani sheikhs) mentioned that they did not know the length and width of al-Qalis. It had a great door made from copper that was ten cubits tall and four cubits wide. The entrance led to an inner building that was 80 cubits long and 40 cubits wide, all decorated with engraved teak wood [saj] with gold and silver nails. This building led to a large court that was 40 cubits long on the right-hand side, and the same on the left-hand side. Its arches were decorated with mosaics with golden stars visible between the columns. The court led to a dome with a diameter of 30 cubits. Its walls were covered with mosaics, and there was a cross engraved with mosaics, gold, and silver. It had a square white and black [balq] marble piece which faced in the direction of the sunrise. Its size was ten cubits on

---

109. Creswell, K. A. C. "IV.—The Ka'ba in A.D. 608." *Archaeologia* 102–97 :(1951) 94. https://doi.org/10.1017/S0261340900007220.

each side. It dazzled the eyes of those who viewed it from the center of the dome, and it let the light of the sun and moon flow inside the dome. Below the marble piece, there was a pulpit made of labkh wood, which was ebony wood decorated with white ivory. The steps of the pulpit were made of teak wood covered with gold and silver. In the dome there were silver chains, and there was in the dome and in the building two ornamented beams of teak wood, 60 cubits long. One of them was called Kua'ib [كعيب], and the other one was called the wife of Kua'ib. During al-Jahiliyya, people used to venerate them. Kua'ib was called al-Ahwazi, which in their language means 'the free man.'

"During the construction of al-Qalis, Abraha was very harsh on the builders. He took an oath to cut off the hand of any builder who did not come to the building site before sunrise."

The narrator said: "one time, a builder stayed behind until after the sunrise. His mother was an old lady and he brought her with him to plead for mercy for her son. She approached Abraha and mentioned to him the reason for her son's delay and asked for his mercy. Abraha said, 'I don't perjure myself, nor jeopardize (the work of) my workers.' Then he gave his orders to cut off the builder's hand. The mother said to Abraha, 'strike metal objects with your hoe; today is yours and tomorrow for others—not forever yours.' Abraha said, 'come closer.' Then he asked her, 'will this monarchy go to someone else?' She said, 'yes.'

"Abraha had planned to raise the building of al-Qalis until he could see the sea of Adan when he climbed to the top. After that, Abraha said, 'I shall not place one more stone,' and he stopped all the construction work.

"The news that Abraha was building al-Qalis has spread among the Arabs. A man from the Nasa'a [النسأة], from Bani-Malik ibn Kinanah, heard about al-Qalis and became very angry. He decided to go to Abraha's building, and when he arrived, he entered al-Qalis and defecated in it. Later, Abraha entered the building and saw what had happened there. He said, 'who did that?' and was told that an Arab man did it. Abraha became outraged and said, 'I shall not stop until I demolish their House in Mecca.'"

The narrator continued: "Abraha marched with an elephant towards Mecca to demolish the House, and so the well-known story of the elephant happened. Al-Qalis remained intact until the time when Abu-Ja'far al-Mansor, the Muslims' caliph, appointed al-Abbas ibn al-Rabi' ibn Ubaydullah al-Harithi to Yaman. It was mentioned to al-Abbas that al-Qalis was full of gold and silver, and that appealed to him. He was told, 'you will gain treasures and lots of money from it.' He was yearning to demolish al-Qalis and take its treasure.

"He sent to Ibn Wahb ibn Munabbih to consult with him about demolishing it. Al-Abbas said, 'I have been advised by several people from al-Yaman not to demolish al-Qalis; I find it difficult to do it with Kua'ib in it. I was told the people of Jahiliyya glorified him and sought his blessing, and that he spoke to them and told them news of what they like and what they fear.' Ibn Wahb said to him, 'all you heard is false. Kua'ib was an idol from the idols of Jahiliyya which fascinated them. Give a command to bring a drum and a flute and use them to energize and delight the demolition workers. You will gain lots of money and, at the same time, you will take revenge against the wrongdoers who had burned (the palace of) Ghumdan. You will also gain the honor of erasing the Habash building from the memory of your people.'

"At Sana'a there was a Jewish scholar. He approached al-Abbas ibn al-Rabi' and said, 'a king who demolishes al-Qalis will rule al-Yaman for 40 years.'"

The narrator continued: "when al-Abbas listened to both opinions, that of the Jewish man and Ibn Wahb ibn Munabbih, he made his decision to demolish al-Qalis."

156 - Abu al-Walid said, the trustworthy one narrated to me, saying:
"I saw al-Abbas demolish al-Qalis, and he gained lots of money from it. Then I saw him giving commands to get chains and tie Kua'ib and the other wooden beam with those chains so they could be dragged outside. No one dared to touch the beams because of their fear of what might happen to whoever dragged them outside, as told by the people of Yaman. Al-Abbas called for al-Wardeen, which are bulls, and they attached the chains to them and dragged the beams, with the help of men.

"When they were outside the walls of al-Qalis, and the people of Yaman witnessed that nothing bad had happened, a man from Iraq who was a merchant in Sana'a came and bought the beams. He cut them to use in his house. After a short time, the man suffered from leprosy. The riffraff said, 'this has happened to him because he bought Kua'ib.'"

The narrator continued: "then I saw the people of Sana'a search around al-Qalis, picking pieces of gold and silver from it."

The narrator then recited what Ibn Ishaq said: "when the Arabs heard about the letter that Abraha sent to al-Najashi, a man from al-Nasa'a (those who change the calendar) from Bani-Faqim from (the tribe of) Bani-Malik ibn Kinanah became very angry and travelled to al-Qalis and he defecated in it. Then he traveled back to his land.

"When Abraha was told about the incident he said, 'who has done that?' He was told, 'an Arabic man from the House at Mecca to which the Arabs go for pilgrimage. When he heard that you intend to divert the Arab pilgrims to [al-Qalis], he became furious, so he came and defecated in it, and by that he aims to say it is not worthy of that purpose.' Abraha then became very angry and swore that he would march to the House and demolish it.

"He prepared his army and marched with an elephant towards Mecca. When the Arabs heard that Abraha wanted to demolish the Ka'ba, the Forbidden House of Allah, they were determined to resist him. One of the noblemen and kings of Yaman called Dhu-Nafar had called on his people and the Arab tribes to fight against Abraha and defend the Forbidden House of Allah. His call was answered by many of them. They faced Abraha and fought against him, but Dhu-Nafar was taken captive. When Abraha wanted to kill him, [Dhu-Nafar] said, 'oh king, do not kill, for keeping me alive could be better for you than killing me.' So Abraha spared his life, but he imprisoned him and chained him up. Abraha was a patient man and had a strong faith in Christianity.

"He continued his march towards the Ka'ba until he reached the land of Khathu'm [خثعم] where he faced resistance from Nufail ibn Habib al-Khatu'mi, with the tribes of Khathu'm Shahran and Nahis and some other Arab tribes. They fought against Abraha, but he defeated them and took Nufail captive. He was brought to Abraha and he said, 'oh king, do not kill me; I can be your guide in the Arab lands, and here are my hands (which I will use) to make sure you have complete obedience from the tribes of Khathu'm Shahran and Nahis.' Abraha pardoned him and spared his life, and he took Nufail with him as a guide.

"When they arrived at al-Ta'if, a man called Masud ibn Miti'b went out to meet Abraha with a group of men from Thaqeef. They said, 'oh king, we are your slaves, obediently listening to you. We have no dispute with you, and our house is not the House you want (they meant al-Lat). What you want is the House in Mecca, and we will send someone with you to guide you to that House.' Abraha pardoned them, and they sent a man called Abu-Raghal with him as a guide. When they arrive at al-Maghmas, Abu-Raghal died there. The Arabs used to pelt the grave of Abu-Raghal with stones. His grave is so well known that even Jarir ibn al-Khatfi (the poet) mentioned it in a poem, saying:

if al-Farazdq died,
then pelt (his grave) with stones as you do with Abu-Raghal.

"While Abraha was still at al-Maghmas, he sent a man from al-Habasha named al-Aswad ibn Mafsud on the back of his horse until he reached the frontiers of Mecca. He managed to seize money from the people of Tahama, who are Quraysh, and other tribes. Among what he seized was 200 camels, which belonged to Abdul-Muttalib ibn Hashim, who was the leader of the Quraysh at that time.

"The tribes of the Quraysh, Khuza'i, Kinanah, Hudhail, and everyone who was at al-Haram were determined to resist Abraha, but they realized that did not have the strength to defeat him. Then Abraha sent a man named Hanatah al-Himyari to Mecca and gave him instructions, saying, 'ask for the leader of those people and the most noble of them, and tell him the king says, "I have not come to fight you, but I only want to demolish this House. Therefore, if you do not resist me, I do not need to shed your blood."' Then Abraha said to the man, 'if he does not want to fight, bring him to me.'

"When Hanatah entered Mecca, he asked for the leader and nobleman of the Quraysh, and he was directed to Abdul-Muttalib. He told him what Abraha said, then Abdul-Muttalib said, 'by Allah, we do not want to fight him, and we have no strength for that. This is the Forbidden House of Allah, and the House of Ibrahim Khalilullah. If Allah prevents him (from harming it), then it is His House and His Sanctuary. And if He allows him to reach It, then, by Allah, we have no power to defend it.' After that Hanatah said to him, 'come with me then, as he ordered me to bring you to him.' Abdul-Muttalib accompanied him with some of his sons to the campsite of Abraha.

"When he reached there, Abdul-Muttalib asked about Dhu-Nafar, as he was his friend, so he visited him in his prison. Abdul-Muttalib said, 'oh Dhu-Nafar, have you got anything to help us in this (calamity) that has descended on us?' Dhu-Nafar said, 'how can a prisoner who is waiting for his death at any time to be of any help? But the only thing I can offer is to send you to my friend Anees, the elephant's stableman, and I will ask him to do all he can for you with the king and to raise your status with him. I will ask him to grant permission for you to approach the king and to talk with him about everything you want to say. He will intercede for you if he can.' Abdul-Muttalib said, 'that would be enough for me.' Dhu-Nafar sent for Anees and said to him, 'Abdul-Muttalib is the chief of the Quraysh, and the owner of the caravans of Mecca. He feeds people in the mountains and the land and feeds the beasts on the mountain tops. The king has seized 200 camels from him. So, ask the permission of the king for him and help him with what you can.' Anees said, 'I will.'

"He talked to Abraha and said, 'oh king, this is the chief of the Quraysh at your door, asking for your permission. He is the owner of the caravans of Mecca and he feeds people in the mountains and the land and feeds the beasts on the mountains tops. I hope that you give him your permission, so he can talk to you about his needs.' Abraha gave him his permission. Abdul-Muttalib was very handsome and a muscular man. When Abraha saw him, he admired and welcomed him. Abraha disliked letting Abdul-Muttalib sit beneath him, and at the same time, he disliked being seen by the Habasha people letting Abdul-Muttalib sit next to him on his bed (throne), so he decided to descend from his bed and sit on the carpet beside Abdul-Muttalib.

"Then Abraha said to his interpreter, 'ask him, what is his need?' The interpreter asked him and Abdul-Muttalib said, 'I need the king to return 200 camels that have been taken from me.' When the interpreter reported to Abraha what Abdul-Muttalib needed, he said, 'tell him, "I admired you when you I saw you, but when you spoke to me I disliked you. You talk about 200 camels that I took from you! And you do not speak to me about a House, which is your religion and the religion of your fathers, and I have come to destroy it—but you do not speak about it?' Abdul-Muttalib replied, 'I am the lord of these camels, and the House has a Lord Who will protect it.' Abraha said, 'no one can protect it from me.' Abdul-Muttalib said, 'then that is your affair.'"

Ibn Ishaq said: "some scholars said that when Abdul-Muttalib went with Hanata al-Himyari to meet Abraha, some other leaders accompanied him. Those were Ya'mur ibn Nufatha ibn Odai ibn Ad-Dail ibn Bakr ibn Abdu-Munat ibn Kinanah, who was the chief of Bani-Bakr at that time, and Khowailid ibn Wathilah al-Hadhli, who was the chief of Hudhail at that time. They offered Abraha one-third of the money of Tahama in return for not demolishing the House. Abraha refused their offer, and Allah knows best whether this story really happened.

"The camels of Abdul-Muttalib were returned to him, and when they left Abraha, Abdul-Muttalib went to the Quraysh and told them the news. He ordered them to evacuate Mecca and seek shelter in the mountain paths, to protect them from the cruelty of Abraha's army. Afterward, Abdul-Muttalib held the jamb of the Ka'ba's door with some other people from the Quraysh and they started praying to Allah the Almighty and asked Him for help against Abraha and his army. Abdul-Muttalib said, while still holding the Ka'ba's door, 'oh Lord, a man should defend his home and You can defend Your Own House. Prevent the fellows of the cross from harming Your House; their power can never overcome Your Power.' After that, Abdul-Muttalib let go of the Ka'ba's door and set off with the rest of the Quraysh to the mountains of Mecca. They took refuge in those mountains and were waiting and anticipating what danger Abraha would be to Mecca when he entered. Abdul-Muttalib also said, 'we are the people of Allah in his city. We remain on the path of Ibrahim, worship Allah, maintain the ties of kinship, and fulfil our promises. The House has a Lord protecting it from whoever intends to harm it.'

"The next morning, Abraha was prepared to enter Mecca. He gave orders to his army to load their supplies and prepare the elephant for him. The elephant's name was Mahmoud. Abraha was determined to demolish the Ka'ba and go back to al-Yaman. When they directed the elephant towards Mecca, Nufail ibn Habib al-Khatu'mi approached the elephant and held his ear and said, 'sit down, Mahmoud, and go back wisely to where you came from. You are in the Sacred place of Allah.' Then he let go of his ear. The elephant sat down, and Nufail ibn Habib climbed the mountain. The men of Abraha beat the elephant to get it to stand up but that did not work. They beat his head with a hatchet, but he refused to stand up. Then they stabbed him with staves in the thin areas of his body but again he did not move. They directed him towards al-Yaman and he went quickly. They directed him towards al-Sham, and then towards the east, and in both ways he went quickly. Again, they directed him towards Mecca, but the elephant sat down.

"Then Allah the Almighty sent birds from the sea that looked like starling birds; each bird carried three stones, one in its beak and two in its legs. The stones were like chickpeas and lentils. If they hit anyone he died immediately, but not everyone was hit. Those who were not hit by the stones fled, searching for their way back to al-Yaman. They asked Nufail ibn Habib to guide them on their way."

Nufail said: "when I saw Allah's wrath that descended on Abraha's army, you forgave me and did not hold harm against me. So I praised God as I saw the birds and was afraid until the stones that were thrown at us lessened, but everyone was asking about the elephant. The army went out, falling one after another along the way, and were destroyed at every waterhole. Abraha's body was injured so they took him out with them. His fingers were falling off, one after another. Every time a fingernail fell off it was followed by pus[110] and blood, until they reached Sana'a, where he was like a helpless young bird.[111] He did not die until he had opened-up about what was in his heart about what they believed. Some remnants of Abraha's army stayed at Mecca; they served and shepherded the sheep for the people of Mecca."

Ibn Ishaq said: "I have been told that rubeola and smallpox were first seen at the Arabian Peninsula that year."

Abu al-Walid and some of the people of Mecca said: "the doves of Mecca first appeared at that time. It is said that these doves are the offspring of the birds that attacked the owners of the elephant.

"After the death of Abraha, his son Yaqsoom ibn Abraha ruled al-Habasha [in Yaman], and after him al-Habasha was ruled by his brother Masrooq ibn Abraha, who was killed by the Persians when Saif ibn Dhi Yazan came to them; [Masrooq] was the last Habashi king. Those who came from al-Habasha were four kings in total and they ruled al-Yaman for 30 years. When Allah the Almighty thwarted the attack of Abraha on Mecca, the Quraysh's status among the Arabs was raised. [The Arabs] said, (referring to the Quraysh), 'those are the people of Allah; He defended them and defeated their enemy.' The Arabs recited several poems describing what Allah did to al-Habasha and described al-Ashram [Abraha] and the elephant and how he wanted to demolish the House of Allah."

> While Ibn Ishaq refers to rubeola and smallpox, Abraha's necrosis of the hands is consistent with the plague of Justinian. The plague of Justinian, caused by the same bacterium as the Black Death, killed an estimated 15-100 million people across the Byzantine empire. If Abraha contracted the plague of Justinian, it would suggest he had traveled further north than Mecca in the Hijaz.

---

110. Or festering matter.
111. It's possible a medical term was intended here.

www.ingramcontent.com/pod-product-compliance
Lightning Source LLC
Chambersburg PA
CBHW060535080526
44586CB00012B/744